Shit Doesn't Just Happen II

The Gift of Failure

Cool Gus Publishing
http://coolgus.com

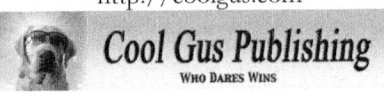

Shit Doesn't Just Happen II

The Gift of Failure

(Challenger, Czar, Sultana, Mulholland, Kursk, Pearl Harbor, Alive!)

Bob Mayer

NOTE FROM THE PUBLISHER

All images used throughout this book are part of the
public domain, or the author has licensed the use of the
image.

CONTENTS

ICONS USED IN THIS BOOK

I use icons in this book to focus on specific parts of the book. They are:

Definitions.

Timeline of each catastrophe.

Asides: When you see the sign below, it means I'm giving you bonus information either based on my personal experience during my time in the military and as a Green Beret or information regarding a similar disaster/event/catastrophe.

THREE REASONS TO READ THIS BOOK

Reason one
False Assumptions

WHAT IS A *CATASTROPHE*?

The final event of the dramatic action, especially of a tragedy

An event causing great and often sudden damage or suffering; a disaster

Utter failure

We are usually surprised when a catastrophe strikes. There is a tendency to believe that a catastrophe is something that is unexpected, always happens suddenly, and is caused by a single thing going wrong.

These are false assumptions. The vast majority of catastrophes can easily be predicted with some attention and focus. If predicted, they can often be planned for and averted. If unavoidable, they can be planned for and their results blunted and minimized. Catastrophes occur suddenly only in terms of the final event, the catastrophe itself; however, the buildup, via a series of what we will term *cascade events*, can be very long in the unfolding. And at least one of these cascade events involves human error. Thus most catastrophes can be avoided.

I will go through seven well-known catastrophes, showing the six cascade events leading to the seventh and *final event*. I will list the events, pointing out how each could either be noted (knowledge often can prevent the cascade of events that lead to #7, the final event) or corrected. The key for us to focus on is what was learned and changed because of each, saving the lives of countless others afterward.

Reason two
A catastrophe is closer than you think

While you might not have personally been in a catastrophe or a tragedy, I can assure you that we have all come close more often than we realize. Many times we've been to a #4, #5 or #6 cascade event and not gone into the final event; therein lies one of the key deceptions that lulls us into complacency.

As we will see in the seven examples, there are many places along the cascade of events where a single person saying or doing something, could have stopped the cascade and prevented the catastrophe. Or, at the very least, minimized the effect of the final event. Thus, it's very important for us to understand how seemingly innocuous events can play a tragic role if left unchecked. This book is also about the *gift of failure*: how we can learn from past catastrophes in order to avoid ones in the future. The aviation industry works off the gift of failure in that practically every safety innovation introduced is developed in response to a plane crash.

Ultimately, it's about gaining the proper catastrophe mindset, which goes against our natural instincts because...

Reason Three
Delusion Events Fool Us

We often look at narrow escapes or near misses as 'fortunate' events where disaster was averted; indeed, we get to the point where we normalize near misses. Instead, we need to look at these 'fortunate' events as cascade events where we came close to catastrophe and were simply lucky that we didn't hit the final event. Relying on luck is a very dangerous mindset yet we immerse ourselves in it on a daily basis. We often call it 'dodging the bullet' forgetting that when a bullet hits, the results are catastrophic to the target.

We need to focus on cascade events, see their negative potential, and reduce their occurrence. A cascade event that doesn't lead to a final event we will label a *delusion event*. A cascade event and delusion event are exactly the same: the only difference is that a delusion event doesn't result in a final event.

This time.

Delusion events lead us into delusional thinking: that we will continue to dodge the bullet by doing nothing. In fact, a delusion event, where something goes wrong, but doesn't lead to the final event, reinforces our complacency to do nothing about correcting a delusion event and increases our risk of a final event, a catastrophe. We take the delusion event as the status quo, not an aberration. Delusion events lead to the normalization of unacceptable risk. For a very simple example, the further you drive with the check engine light on in your car, the more you think it's normal for that light to be on. Diane Vaughan calls this normalization in her book The Challenger Launch Decision. (1) We'll discuss this catastrophe as one of our seven in the second book in this series, focusing on organizational thinking about delusion events.

How many times have you been in a hotel or restaurant or store and the fire alarm goes off? How many times did you hurry to the exit? Rather, didn't you, and everyone around you, with no smoke or fire noted, stand around, and wait for someone to actually announce what's going on? We've been desensitized by false alarms to the point where the alarm serves little purpose any more.

The Harvard Business Review did a study in 2011 (2) and found that delusion events (multiple near misses) preceded every disaster and business crisis they studied over a seven-year period. Besides delusional thinking leading to normalization, the other problem is outcome bias. If you flip a coin six times and it comes up heads six times, even though statistically rare (1 chance in 64 attempts), you will tend to start focusing on the result, believing all coin tosses end up heads. While we know this isn't true, we tend to base our probabilities of future occurrences not on the statistics of reality but on our experiences.

This is called heuristics and is at the root of many disasters. *Heuristics* is experience-based techniques for learning and problem solving that give a solution, which isn't necessarily optimal. We generalize based on the things we value most: our own experience and information related to us from sources we trust. Think how many 'truths' you have heard that turn out to be nothing more than an urban legend or a superstition. Yet, we base many of our daily and emergency actions around these.

A small example from *The Green Beret Survival Guide*: every so often there is a news article about someone in a desperate survival situation who claims drinking their urine helped them make it through. That's absolutely the wrong thing to do. But it's one of those stories that is repeated enough, until we believe it to be true. Because we only hear from survivors, who lived in spite of doing the wrong thing.

It is human nature that we focus on successful outcomes much more than negative ones. It's irrational, but that's part of being human. In the same way, managers and leaders are taught to plan for success, not failure, since it's believed planning for failure is negative thinking. In fact, I would submit that many people are part of a cult of positive thinking that often excludes reality.

The good news is we tend to be predictably irrational and understanding our tendency to make a cascade event a delusion event, is the first step in correcting this problem.

At the end of this book, I discuss THE RULE OF SEVEN and THE THREE BENEFITS OF CATASTROPHE THINKING, PLANNING & PREPARING. Many of the definitions below come from there.

DEFINITION: Shit Happens: life is full of unpredictable events and there's nothing we can do about it. Bad things happen to people for no particular reason.

DEFINITION: No-do-over: An event that can't be undone, often where death or serious is involved.

DEFINITION: Catastrophe:
The final event of the dramatic action, especially of a tragedy
An event causing great and often sudden damage or suffering; a disaster
Utter failure

DEFINITION: The Rule of 7: rarely does a disaster happens in isolation or as the result of a single event. It usually requires a minimum of 7 things to go wrong in order for a catastrophe. And one of those 7 is always human error.

DEFINITION: Cascade Event: An event prior to a catastrophe that contributes to the actual catastrophe, but by itself, is not catastrophic.

DEFINITION: Final Event: A catastrophic event. The culmination of at least six cascade events.

DEFINITION: The Gift of Failure: how we can learn from past catastrophes in order to avoid ones in the future.

DEFINITION: Delusion Event: A cascade event that doesn't lead to a final event.

DEFINITION: Heuristics: experience based techniques for problem solving, learning and discovery that gives solutions not guaranteed to be optimal.

DEFINITION: Lose-lose scenarios: This is a training scenario where there is no 'right' solution.

DEFINITION: Catastrophe mindset: Expecting that what can go wrong; will.

DEFINITION: HALO: Looking at something from 'outside the box' gives one a fresh and unique perspective.

DEFINITION: Delusional mindset. Someone who has had success far beyond that which should be the norm, helped with an abnormal amount of luck, believe the abnormal is normal and that their streak will continue indefinitely.

DEFINITION: House Rules: The problem with playing by your own rules is that reality ultimately catches up to you. No person is larger than the world around them. Reality trumps a delusional mindset.

DEFINITION: Cascade Stopper: A person designated as the check and balance on a leader, especially under stressful situations.

DEFINITON: Self-correcting mindset. This is where we shrug off a physical symptom or an anomaly in our environment and just assume it will get better.

Definition: *Sunk cost* is a past cost that has already been incurred and cannot be recovered. It should not be a factor in current decision-making.

REFERENCES

Diane Vaughan The Challenger Launch Decision: Risky Technology, Culture and Deviancy at NASA, University of Chicago Press (April 15, 1997) http://www.amazon.com/The-Challenger-Launch-Decision-Technology/dp/0226851761/ref=sr_1_1?ie=UTF8&qid=1408310530&sr=8-1&keywords=the+challenger+launch+decision

Harvard Business Review: How To Avoid Catastrophe; Catherine H. Tinsley, Robin L. Dillon, and Peter M. Madsen. April 2011. http://hbr.org/2011/04/how-to-avoid-catastrophe/ar/1

CATASTROPHE I: THE *CHALLENGER*
Organizational Failure

"My God, Thiokol. When do you want me to launch? Next April?" Senior NASA official on a conference call to the manufacturer of the solid boosters, when they recommended on the morning of the launch that it be postponed.

It is rare that we get to see a catastrophe as it actually happens. Usually, we see the end result, the wreckage, and perhaps (but rarely in our correct society) the bodies. When the space shuttle *Challenger* exploded on 28 January 1986, millions of people were watching live as it was also the first time a civilian, a school teacher, was being sent into space. Those not watching live were able to quickly see taped replays.

There are some things that weren't seen or understood. One was the likelihood that the crew survived the initial explosion and remained alive for two minutes and forty-five seconds until the intact crew compartment impacted with the water. To this day, this is something that NASA goes to pains to minimize.

Challenger is a classic example of Cascade Events, any of which could have easily been stopped, saving the lives of the seven on the craft and preventing an almost fatal blow to our space program. Additionally, the fact NASA truly did not take to heart the Cascade Events during an After Action Review (discussed under 7 Ways to Prevent Catastrophes included at the end of the book) led to a second shuttle disaster when the *Columbia* broke up as it re-entered Earth atmosphere in 2003.

The Facts

On 28 January 1986, the Space Shuttle *Challenger* broke into pieces 73 seconds into flight due to a failure in the O-Ring seal on the right solid booster on liftoff. This failure allowed hot gas from the inside of the booster to impinge the booster attachment and external fuel tank. The booster separated and the external tank failed, leading to the break up of the orbiter.

All seven crewmembers died. The exact moment of their deaths is unknown, as the crew compartment remained intact after the break up until impact with the ocean two minutes and forty-five seconds later. Evidence indicates at least one of them was conscious during this long fall.

15 January 1986: Flight readiness review. *Challenger* is given a go.

22-24 January 1986: Original launch window is missed because of delays from previous mission. Launch is rescheduled for 27 January.

26 January 1986: A cold front sweeps across Florida.

27 January 1986: Launch is delayed due to issues with a safety lock, then high winds.

28 January 1986: *Challenger* launches. 73 seconds into flight it explodes.

28 January 1986: President Reagan delays his State of the Union and makes a speech regarding the *Challenger* tragedy.

The Cascading Events

Cascade One

The focus during development of the space shuttle was on the shuttle's main engines and the tiles, not the boosters. The 31,000 tiles had to absorb the heat of re-entry and then be used again and again. As *Columbia* would show, the integrity of these tiles was crucial to the integrity of the spaceship itself. The three shuttle engines had to deliver more power in a smaller package than any previous engines had ever done.

It's natural that in the development of the shuttle, NASA would be focused on these two areas. While two solid rocket boosters would be used, the technology in them was considered pretty basic and time-tested. A solid rocket booster is relatively simple, with solid fuel housed in a half-inch thick steel tube. The only moving part was that which maneuvered the exhaust nozzle.

Except it wasn't that simple. The boosters were contracted to Morton Thiokol, which built them in Utah. Thus, the large boosters couldn't be shipped in one piece to the Kennedy Space Center in Florida. They had to be broken into four pieces in order to be transferred by rail.

And therein begins the problem.

After being shipped, the four sections were put together in Florida. Each connection was called a field joint, because it was assembled outside of the factory, which is a red flag. Four sections equal three field joints. The boosters were designed to be reusable so these joints couldn't be welded, since they had to be shipped back to Utah to be refilled with solid propellant after each flight. Without going into extensive detail on how these field joints were constructed, a critical component were two rubber O-rings as a final seal to keep flame from leaking out. The O-rings were then further sealed with putty.

NASA didn't have much concern over the solid rocket boosters (SRB). They were simply enlarging already tested technology that was used in the Titan 3 rocket. In fact, NASA used that as a selling point in their public announcements, saying that they were minimizing experimentation in this component. "Solid rocket, solid technology," was the way it was phrased at a press conference.

The rubber used was developed in World War II to line the fuel tanks of aircraft so that they had limited leakage after being punctured by gunfire. The rubber worked fine as long as it wasn't too cold. They tested it down to 36 degrees, below what the manufacturer considered a safe temperature.

Lesson

We often focus on what we perceive to be the major obstacles and in doing so, neglect potential hazards.

NASA never tested the SRBs under liftoff conditions until the first shuttle launch.

Since it worked fine then, this led to . . .

Cascade Two

The booster had never burned through before; therefore, it wouldn't in the future.

A classic series of delusion events, to the point where the danger was no longer considered a danger. Enough of a delusion to lead to Cascade Event Six below.

Four years before the first shuttle flight, NASA engineers began exhibiting concern about the field joints. Memos (the glaring red and white flag of danger) were circulated that the joints might fail at the extreme pressures of ignition. A *red and white flag of danger* is when a potential problem is noted, but little action is taken. The person noting the danger feels as if they've accomplished something by writing the memo, when in reality, it only shifts responsibility but doesn't fix the problem. Thus, it's running up a red flag of danger while at the same time waving a white flag of helplessness and passing of responsibility. Often a memo written or a task force formed becomes a delusion event in that they make us believe we are solving a problem just by doing the memo or forming the task force.

But then the first ten shuttle flights went off without any problem.

Problem solved.

Not exactly. In essence, the O-rings were never really tested on those flights because flame rarely got past the putty to the rings. But then, more signs showed up that gas was reaching the O-rings, most likely as a result of a new test procedure that used nitrogen gas to test the rings. Most disturbingly, some burn marks reached the second, final, O-ring. In essence, danger was down to the last check.

In January of 1985, during a mission of the Discovery, five O-rings were discovered to be damaged. NASA responded by putting together a task force, which ranks just above the memo in terms of red and white flag of dangers. They made some recommendations, but obviously, not enough.

The shuttle continued to fly and the successful flight of the Discovery, despite the burns, indicated a cold-weather launch really wasn't such a dangerous thing after all. Right?

Lesson

Delusion events are just that. The Discovery burns launched a task force but there was no real change; indeed the success of the cold weather flight of Discovery was a major delusion event. And was ignored the following year when Challenger was set to take off in even colder weather. The five burnt O-rings should have brought things to a screeching halt, but launch pressures negated bringing the shuttle program to a screeching halt.

A catastrophe would have to do that.

Cascade Three

Tests of the boosters were done statically, never simulating actual flight.

Using the solid rocket technology similar to that used in the Titan and other missiles cut down on the amount of testing NASA had Morton-Thiokol do on the SRBs. They only ran seven trials, and not a single one under the torque that the booster would experience during an actual launch.

In actual launch conditions, the seemingly solid SRBs were subject to tremendous torque and bending. First, when the shuttle engines ignited, just before the SRBs, the entire ensemble bent almost three feet and then snapped forward. That's a significant stressor. Next, there were the stress points at the struts where the SRBs were attached to the shuttle's main fuel tank. Not considering these factors was a serious oversight.

Lesson

Tests have to be made under real conditions as much as possible. Once more, we have a factor that became a delusion event with each successful shuttle mission.

Cascade Four

Political, budget and scheduling issues led to a high-pressure atmosphere to push ahead, sacrificing safety in the process.

The Space Shuttle program was born as the Apollo program was winding down. NASA was under pressure as its budget was being cut to a third of that at the height of Apollo, to come up with a way to continue its programs in a cost effective way. A reusable shuttle could cut the cost of putting a payload into space to $1/20^{th}$ of what it was. There was even speculation the program could turn a profit by contracting to civilian corporations to launch their satellites. (There were those in the Reagan administration who were so optimistic, that they were contacting airlines to get information on how to run a commercial space venture, much like an airline).

Facing constant budget battles and cuts, NASA was under pressure to have a reliable schedule for shuttle launches in order to fulfill orders from its satellite customers. Despite having four shuttles, NASA was falling behind the demand. Where it had been able to set its own launch pace during Apollo, NASA had made a deal with the devil of commerce and was under obligation to its customers.

Pressing on the Challenger launch wasn't this mission on 28 January, but the follow on one for the same shuttle when it was to deploy the Ulysses probe, a major project. Ulysses had to go up by 15 May in order to make its appointed rendezvous.

The evening of 28 January, President Ronald Reagan was scheduled to give his State of the Union. The Challenger mission was the first to have a civilian on board, Christa McAuliffe, the first 'teacher in space.' There is no doubt that this event was to be part of Reagan's address. While there is no direct evidence of influence from the White House, there is no doubt that NASA's hierarchy was aware of the implications. The desire to please the boss, especially the boss that oversees the budget, is a reality in all workplaces.

Lesson

Safety concerns often fall prey to scheduling and external politics and Standing Operating Procedures need to be implemented in order to prevent such pressure from causing bad decisions. While speed kills, it kills in more than just the immediate sense. A pressure to keep to an unrealistic schedule can cause people into poor decision-making and feed delusional thinking.

Speed kills is a recurring theme in these books, and it works in many different way. From actual speed, such as the Titanic, to bureaucratic speed as happened here.

SOPs, which we'll talk about in Ways to Prevent, are critical in the decision making process. They help remove the burden from the final decision maker and creates a solid fallback position in the case of a no-go.

Cascade Five

No astronaut was part of the conference call regarding the O-Rings, nor was any in on the final launch decision.

"Nothing is impossible to the man who doesn't have to do it." That was one of my A-Team sergeant's favorite sayings and actually part of his policy letter in our team SOP.

During the build up to the launch, and during the conference call noted next in Cascade Six, no astronaut was involved or consulted. I have little doubt that if any of the crew of Challenger had been present at the conference call, they would have made strenuous objections to the decision to over-ride the concerns of the Thiokol engineers regarding the booster and a cold weather launch.

In Special Forces, we sometimes received a mission tasking invented by someone who obviously had no idea how we operated or what the realities of the Area of Operations were. While it seems that involving the operators in the tasking might lead to conflict and negativity, often it leads to more efficient ways to do things.

In the early days of the postal service when they began using aircraft, pilots started to complain that they were ordered into the air by dispatchers, despite the weather being marginal or worse than marginal for flying. The dispatchers were under great pressure to maintain the timeliness of the mail deliveries. Safety was secondary to them, but not to the pilots. A policy was implemented where the dispatcher had to take off and do a circuit around the airfield at the behest of the pilot, if the pilot felt the weather was risky.

Not surprisingly, dispatchers became less likely to send pilots aloft into adverse weather.

Lesson

Those who do, help decide. Involve an operator in the decision making process. Involve someone who has to live with the results of the decision.

NASA did make a change in policy after Challenger. An astronaut was involved in every launch, with the ultimate authority to decide whether or not the countdown could proceed. Not only was an astronaut given that power, but also he was involved in the process up to launch day, sitting in on all meetings (such as the conference call in the next cascade). He could bring up questions and issues and make sure they were satisfactorily resolved.

Cascade Six

A recommendation from the boosters' manufacturer not to launch wilted away under NASA pressure.

Roger Boisjoly was a Thiokol engineer who worked on the SRBs. Six months before the Challenger event; he sent a memo to his managers predicting a "catastrophe of the highest order" involving "loss of human life" during a cold weather launch. He pointed directly at the O-rings as the linchpin for disaster.

The day before the launch, seeing the forecast for a launch time temperature of 30 degrees, Boisjoly and four other engineers realized it was too dangerous to launch the next morning. They knew for certain that if the O-rings failed, and they would, that the shuttle was doomed.

Relaying their recommendation to their management team, and arguing their position for hours, it led to an 8:45 conference call on the morning of the 28th between Thiokol managers and NASA managers.

The Thiokol managers recommended against a launch, which led to a severe reaction from the NASA end. George Hardy of NASA: "I am appalled. I am appalled by your recommendation."

The shuttle program manager, Lawrence Mulloy, followed this with: "My God, Thiokol. When do you want me to launch? Next April?"

In the face of this, Thiokol managers reconsidered and gave their approval, over-riding their own engineers and experts.

Boisjoly and the four other engineers watched the launch at their plant. They fully expected the seals to fail on the launch pad and the craft never to lift off at all. When it did, there was a sense of relief. After one minute, one turned to the others and said: "Oh God. We made it. We made it!"

Thirteen second later *Challenger* blew up.

Curiously, until NPR uncovered Boisjoly and the other engineers and got this story, these personnel weren't even interviewed by the special commission investigating the Challenger catastrophe.

Lesson

Managers and leaders shouldn't be able to over-ride experts.

The managers at NASA were working off delusional thinking, since every other launch, including Discovery the previous January in cold weather, had succeeded. The managers at Thiokol allowed themselves to be bullied into accepting NASA's delusion. They rationalized for the sake of bureaucratic goals.

They ignored the strong advice of the experts who conclusively stated the joints would fail. There has to be a redline protocol in place to allow experts to overrule their bosses when they know the redline will be crossed.

Final Event

73 seconds after lift off, the right SRB broke free, initiating the disintegration of Challenger.

The flight was doomed from the moment NASA agreed to launch. But, in reality, it was doomed long before that as the cascade events indicate.

Lesson

While the ultimate cause of this catastrophe was a mechanical failure, every Cascade Event involved human decision-making. Thus every one of the six could have been avoided.

During the hearing of the Rogers Commission, physicist Richard Feynman made the point most dramatically during a televised hearing by placing a piece of the rubber into a glass of cold water, then removing it and showing how brittle it became.

While that was the tip of the iceberg, Feynman and the commission were stunned to uncover the disconnect between managers and engineers regarding the shuttle. Some of it was so fundamental that it makes this point most clearly. NASA had what they called a Probabilistic Risk Analysis (PRA). This is a determination of the odds of a disaster. Unfortunately, two parts of the same organization were very far apart on the PRA for a shuttle catastrophe.

Managers believed the chance of a catastrophic failure for the shuttle was 1 in 100,000. But NASA's engineers had calculated it was 1 in 200. That's a difference on a magnitude of 5,000! Yet, NASA used the 1 in 100,000 figure as part of their recruiting tool for Christa McAuliffe. After all, the lifetime odds of being killed in a car accident are 1 in 100 (source: Live Science; http://www.livescience.com/3780-odds-dying.html). According to NASA managers' numbers, you were safer on the shuttle than your odds of being killed by lightning in your lifetime, which is 1 in 83,930.

Feynman summed up his findings thusly: "For a successful technology, reality must take precedence over public relations, for nature cannot be fooled."

NASA buried the parts of the shuttle recovered at sea in two minuteman silos and sealed them with concrete. This was symbolic of NASA's overall attitude, because in 2003, the shuttle Discovery would become the next casualty to a bureaucratic attitude. But that's a story for a future Shit Doesn't Just Happen book.

DEFINITION: Red and white flag of danger is when a potential problem is noted, but little action is taken. The person noting the danger feels as if they've accomplished something by writing the memo, when in reality, it only shifts responsibility but doesn't fix the problem. Thus it means running up a red flag of danger while at the same time waving a white flag of helplessness and passing of responsibility. This often takes the guise of a memo or a task force.

DEFINITION: Redline protocols are written that allow experts to overrule their bosses when they know the redline will be crossed and a catastrophe will result.

CATASTROPHE 2: THE LAST CZAR
Leadership Failure

Quote: "I am not prepared to be a Czar. I never wanted to become one. I know nothing of the business of ruling." Nicholas II, last Czar of Russia.

We still feel the effects of this catastrophe a century later. Few events have changed the course of modern history more than the Russian Revolution and the man most responsible for it was Nicholas II, the last Czar.

THE FACTS

Nicholas II became Czar of Russia in 1896. He led his country into 2 disastrous wars, both of which were lost. He also presided at a time of great social unrest as the traditional serf system was breaking down during the technological revolution. He eventually abdicated in the face of unrelenting pressure, throwing Russia into an intense civil war between the Whites and the Reds, which led to his execution (along with that of his family) and the rise of the communist Soviet Union.

19 May 1868: Nicholas II is born

20 Oct 1894: Alexander III dies and Nicholas II becomes Ruler

14 November 1894: Nicholas II marries Alexandra

14 May 1896: Nicholas II is crowned Czar of Russia; over 1,000 die in a stampede at the celebration festival for the

people; that evening Nicholas attends the French ambassador's gala

8 February 1904: The Russo-Japanese war begins with a sneak attack by the Japanese on the Russian Fleet at Port Arthur

15 October 1904: The Russian Baltic Fleet begins a journey halfway around the world to reinforce the remains of their Far East fleet

27-28 May 1905: The Russian fleet is defeated at the Battle of Tsushima

9 January 1905: Bloody Sunday starts the Russian Revolution

27 June 1905: The *Potemkin* mutiny

5 September 1905: Treaty of Portsmouth ends the Russo-Japanese War; Russia lost the war

17 October 1905: The October Manifesto promises civil liberties and a parliament

15 July 1914: World War I begins

5 September 1915: Nicholas II assumes command of the Russian Army

17 December 1916: Rasputin is murdered

23-27 February 1917: The February Revolution begins

2 March 1917: Czar Nicholas II abdicates

17 July 1918: Nicholas II and his family are executed

The Cascading Events

Cascade One

Nicholas II wasn't properly trained or prepared to lead his country. While his father, Alexander III, was busy ruling Russia a close circle picked by his father, including Constantine Pobedonstev, tutored Nicholas II. They shaped Nicholas II's attitudes, which were counter to what was going on in many other places in the world. Nicholas came to believe that the ruler was supreme and the Czar led by divine right. The Russian Orthodox Church was integral to the country. And Jews were to be hated. A telling statement was Pobedonstev saying that Russia should be 'frozen in time'. This could be considered a rallying cry for those who resist change.

Besides the slanted beliefs and information he received, Nicholas II's personality was not suited to leadership. He was easily swayed and impressionable. He was weak-willed and loath to make decisions, a key trait a Czar, or any leader, needs.

His father recognized these shortcomings, but did little about it, as Alexander III expected to rule for several more decades and believed there would be time for Nicholas to learn what he needed in order to succeed him after the heir turned 30.

Alexander was wrong about the timing of his own death.

Lesson

Preparation and training are key for successful leadership.

Many have argued whether leaders are made or born. In the case of the Czar, he was born into a leadership position. Whether he had the traits born with that is questionable, one of the major drawbacks of a monarchy.

Nicholas II needed to learn a lot, especially as the turn of the century was a time of great technological change and social turmoil. Even if he had learned to lead well with a 'business as usual' Czar attitude, that would not have sufficed. Revolutions and Civil Wars had torn apart America and Europe for over a century, and unrest was now seeping into Russia, which had an antiquated serf system, not suited for the technological revolution.

At the exact time, that Russia needed a thoughtful and decisive leader; they received the exact opposite when Nicholas II took command at age 26. As the following cascade events show, Nicholas II proceeded to make poor decision after poor decision.

Cascade Two

The Russo-Japanese War was a disaster for Russia & particularly Czar Nicholas II.

Later in this book, I'm going to point out that the Japanese *prior-to-war-declared* assault on Port Arthur foreshadowed what happened at Pearl Harbor. Three hours before they declared war on Russia, the Japanese attacked the Russian fleet anchored at Port Arthur and crippled it.

It would only get worse from there for the Russians.

With the Far East fleet crippled, Nicholas II decided to send his Baltic Fleet to the Pacific. One only has to look at a map to question this decision. Add in the fact that the English wouldn't allow passage of the Suez Canal after the Russians had mistakenly fired on some British trawlers, and the Fleet would have sail halfway around the world in order to just get to the battle zone.

It took the Baltic Fleet eight months to sail to the Pacific.

Port Arthur had already fallen, so the Fleet tried to make it to Vladivostok undetected. They almost made it. The Fleet was blacked out, trying to slip through the Tsushima Strait, which goes between Korea and Japan. Except for a Russian hospital, ship that had its lights on in compliance with the rules of war, which negated the blackout, the rest of the fleet was operating under.

Things went downhill from there. At the end of the naval engagement, the Russian Fleet was essentially destroyed in one engagement and the war was lost.

To get an idea how this reverberated throughout Russia, by May 1905, the Black Sea Fleet had been stripped of experienced sailors and officers to join the doomed Baltic Fleet. When word reached the Fleet of the defeat at the battle of Tsushima Strait, morale plummeted. Activists spread dissension on the ranks.

On 27 June 1905, the crew of the battleship *Potemkin* revolted when they were served a meal of borscht made with meat infested with maggots. The ship's captain was killed and the mutineers took over the ship.

This was a microcosm of what was developing in Russia.

Lesson

Regimes rise and fall as wars are won and lost. Critical decisions such as going to war, and how to conduct the war, require decisive leadership, which also realizes when it is over-reaching.

Not only did Russia lose the war, they lost to an enemy that at the time was considered 'inferior' by the European powers; a humiliation piled on top of defeat. It greatly diminished the Czar's image.

There are some who believe that Russia's defeat indirectly destabilized the balance of power in Europe and led to the events that started the First World War. And looking even further, it could be argued that Japan's victory built up a false sense of success that a generation later would lead to the sneak attack on Pearl Harbor and the Second World War in the Pacific.

The defeat certainly damaged the Czar's relationship with the Navy and the Russian Armed Forces. And a monarch relies on the military in order to stay in power.

Cascade Three

Nicholas II's attempts at reform went awry.

Early in the 20th Century, the world was going through the technological revolution. Even in Russia, long an agrarian society, the base was shifting. People were moving to the cities seeking work.

Numerous groups sprang up to represent a restless society. One of the key groups was the Russian Socialist Democratic Party of which Lenin was a member. Groups of workers banded together in the cities to represent their interests.

On the other end of the economic spectrum, some of the wealthy who had traveled outside the country and seen the societal and economic changes in other countries came to believe Russia had to change in order to remain relevant. Nicholas II was caught in a whirlwind of interests that wanted change, but often in different directions.

Lesson

Leaders have to change with the time or else they will be overwhelmed.

Nicholas II wanted Russia to be frozen in the flow of history and in the face of technological and societal upheaval. This put him directly in conflict with significant portions of his subjects.

This all boiled over in 1905 during the Russo-Japanese War. A petition was organized in St. Petersburg asking for an end to the war, formation of an elected Parliament, and more pay with less working hours. Over one hundred thousand people signed the petition and proceeded to march toward the Winter Palace.

The Czar was not present at the palace, but in his name, troops were called out. This led to . . .

Cascade Four

Bloody Sunday was the beginning of the end.

Calling in troops to face the marchers signaled that the Czar was not interested in negotiating change. It grew worse when the troops fired on the marchers. The official death count was 92. The marchers were stopped, but their dispersal from St. Petersburg across the country simply spread their ideas.

At this point, a decision had been made, but it was not one that Nicholas II was completely committed to. Nicholas II wrote in his diary: *"Difficult day! In St. Petersburg there were serious disturbances due to the desire of workers to get to the Winter Palace. The troops had to shoot in different places of the city; there were many dead and wounded. Lord, how painful and bad!"*

These are not the words of someone committed to suppressing change. If this was how Nicholas II truly felt, he should have met the marchers, not had troops fire on them. Instead he felt one way, but allowed his underlings to act in another. For the next decade, until he abdicated, Nicholas II kept going back on forth on dealing with those fomenting change. At times he tried to placate them, at other times he battled them. In the end, he ended up pleasing no one.

The leader of the march on Bloody Sunday published a letter stating in part: *"Nicholas Romanov, formerly Czar and at present soul-murderer of the Russian empire. The innocent blood of workers, their wives and children lies forever between you and the Russian people. May all the blood which must be spilled fall upon you, you Hangman. I call upon all the socialist parties of Russia to come to an immediate agreement among themselves and bring an armed uprising against Czarism."*

Lesson

Half-measures avail us nothing.

This is a popular saying of rehabilitation but it applies to many situations. I am not advocating that Nicholas should have completely suppressed change. That would be fighting the inevitable. But he needed to decide on a course of action and implement it completely. What he ended up doing was slowly giving up power without a cohesive strategy, leading Russia down a path of defeat which then descended the country into a brutal Civil War.

Reviewing the situation one sees Nicholas II focusing on tactical issues without ever having a strategic plan for the course of the country he led. Many Russians were confused about his actions, making them fodder for energetic leaders of various movements who did have a plan and an agenda.

It's hard for people to support a leader when they don't know what he or she stands for. In Ranger School, it's taught that a leader must make a decision during a crisis; even if it's the wrong decision, it's better than doing nothing and getting overwhelmed.

Cascade Five

Czarina Alexandra alienated many.

Nicholas II's choice of a foreign wife didn't little to enhance his status among the Russian people. Alexandra was the granddaughter of Queen Victoria and part of the German Imperial Family, known as *Alix of Hesse and by Rhine* before marriage.

Nicholas II's parents were initially against the marriage, believing that Alix did not make a good impression on the Russian people. Queen Victoria also initially opposed the match.

In retrospect, they were right.

Even in a democracy, a spouse is seen as a critical component of a leader; in a monarchy, the role is critical not just in terms of being the spouse of the ruler, but also in producing an heir for succession. Because Alix was of royal blood, she also carried the gene for the 'royal disease': hemophilia.

After the marriage, Alexandra bore Nicholas II four daughters before producing a son and heir in 1904: Alexei. Who had the royal disease. Which Nicholas II and Alexandra decided to keep a secret from those outside of their inner circle. In essence, the office of the Czar had its future invested in an heir who was unlikely to grow into adulthood. Instead of facing this head on and dealing with the issue, they chose to hide it not just from the public, but in a way from themselves. Besides the duplicity, the nature of Alexei's illness weighed heavily on the royal couple, particularly Alexandra.

Things peaked in 1912 when Alexei was given Last Rites after being injured. Desperate, Alexandra turned to a mystic, Rasputin. He predicted that Alexei would not die. When this turned out to be true, Alexandra began to rely more and more on him, and in a way, so did the Czar.

This alienated many in the Czar's inner circle, an inevitable effect given the constant jockeying for power in an Imperial Court. In a way, Rasputin's influence became a lightning rod for those on all sides who were against the Czar.

Lesson

Personal issues have great effect on the course of events, especially during crisis.

In modern times, we can look at the Monica Lewinsky scandal and the fallout from it as having an indirect effect on the President's focus on Osama Bin Laden and similar threats.

We've all experienced personal turmoil that affected our professional lives. Nicholas II and his wife's personal lives were entwined with their professional lives. There were those who felt Alexandra exerted too much influence on her husband. When she began to be influenced by the mystic Rasputin, this troubled many.

Rasputin's power in the court increased when Nicholas decided to take command of the military during . . .

Cascade Six

World War I was a disaster for Russia & particularly Nicholas II after he assumed supreme command.

World War I broke out in August 1914. Eventually the two sides became the Central Powers (Germany, Austria-Hungary, the Ottoman Empire, and Bulgaria) versus the Allies (consisting primarily of the United Kingdom, France, Italy, and Russia and eventually the United States).

Initially, most Russians rallied to the Czar in a spirit of nationalism. Faced with an outside enemy, many agitators stood down, putting the country first. While war is unfortunate, it offers the leader a chance to unite the country.

If it is prosecuted properly.

Unfortunately, since the defeat in the Russo-Japanese War, while the Russian Army was massive in numbers, its training and equipment were subpar, especially going up against the most modern army in the world in the form of the Germans.

Nicholas II changed the name of the capital, St. Petersburg to Petrogard since the former was considered too German. Which is odd since his wife *was* German.

The Russian Army gained some initial success, but then was defeated at the Battle of Tannenburg. Losses and defeats piled up. Within a year of the beginning of the war, the Germans had conquered Poland and were moving into the Ukraine.

Effects were compounded at home, where there weren't enough men to bring in the harvest. Rationing was imposed, something that never goes over with the populace, especially when all the news from the front was negative.

Desperate, Nicholas II made a decision, one that was obviously foolish to everyone but himself. He relieved the commander of the army and put himself in charge. He did so having no military experience and very little training. It was perhaps a sign of desperation or of narcissism or a combination. Worse, by going to the front, he left his wife in command in the capital, and it was during this time that she was under the influence of Rasputin.

Needless to say, Nicholas II wasn't successful in the prosecution of the war and casualties and defeats piled up. Shortages at home became more extreme and the country, once behind the war, turned against it, and those who sought revolution saw that the opportunity was here.

The Czar's advisers pleaded with him to end the war, but having suffered one defeat in the Russo-Japanese War, he knew his reign could not suffer another.

Lesson

Leadership in one area is not easily transferable to another.

Nicholas II wasn't a very good Czar; for him to think he could be a good military commander was a double negative stroke. Faced with internal unrest, the gamble to enter into World War I was a very high stakes one. If Russia succeeded, he might be able to unite the country. But if the army failed in battle, which would be pouring gasoline on the unrest not only at home, but in the military with whom he already had strained relations after the Russo-Japanese War. By taking command of the military, he alienated the officer corps. By leading the military into defeat after defeat, he destroyed the support of the one group he would need most in case of revolt.

Nicholas II was now considered directly responsible for every defeat.

Finally, troops sent to repress revolting citizens refused to fire on the crowds and joined the revolt. Nicholas tried to reach Petrogard to address the situation, but the route was blocked. On the advice of his generals, he abdicated.

Final Event

Nicholas II and his family are executed. The Last Czar.

Even now, with things critical, Nicholas was not decisive. In book one I talked about the tipping point during the Donner Party, when the decision to turn back needed to be made and wasn't. Having abdicated, Nicholas's priority should have been to get out of Russia and take his family to safety.

His first cousin, King George V of England, refused to allow the Czar and his family sanctuary, concerned about how it would reflect on his own throne.

Nicholas has so alienated not only the people, but also the military. No one would come to his aide as Russia descended into civil war.

Eventually on 17 July 1918, early in the morning, the Czar, his family and some retainers were executed. The bodies were not found until the late 20th century.

Lesson

One man's lack of leadership changed the course of history and dictated the fates of millions.

The rise of the Soviet Union out of the ashes of Czarist Russia is one of the most significant developments in the past century. Lenin, Stalin, purges, the spread of communism, the Cold War where we came perilously close to nuclear war; all were a result of Nicholas.

There were numerous cascade events spread out over decades, but a recurring them of Nicholas II is the lack of decisive leadership along with little strategic political or military planning. He spent much of his reign reacting.

Leadership, or the lack thereof, affects many, from the troopers of the Seventh Cavalry who went to their doom to the estimated 50 million 'unnatural deaths' suffered by Russians under Stalin.

CATASTROPHE 3: THE *SULTANA*
Explosion and Sinking

"If we arrive safe at Cairo it would be the greatest trip ever made on the western waters, as there were more people on board than were ever carried on one boat on the Mississippi River!" William J. Gambrel, first clerk & part owner of the steamship Sultana.

The sinking of the *Sultana* was the greatest maritime disaster in United States history, yet most people have never heard of it. Even at the time of its occurrence, the headline was buried because John Wilkes Booth had been killed the day before the ship went down. In fact, the entire month of April was full of headlines: On the 9th of April 1865, Lee surrendered to Grant at Appomattox Courthouse. On the 14th, President Lincoln was assassinated.

THE FACTS

On 27 April 1865, three of four boilers on board the *Sultana* exploded, killing approximately 1,800. This was a greater loss of life than the Titanic. Most of those killed were Union soldiers, who were former prisoners of war returning home.

This occurred on the Mississippi River, roughly eight miles north of Memphis in the middle of the night.

21 April 1965: *Sultana* departs New Orleans

24 April 1865: *Sultana* arrives at Vicksburg; boiler is 'repaired'. The boat is overloaded, mostly with former Union POWs

26 April 1865: *Sultana* docks at Memphis

27 April 1865: *Sultana* explodes

The Cascading Events

Cascade One

Faulty and hasty repairs on a boiler.

The *Sultana* was a relatively new vessel, built in 1863. Her normal crew was 85. Her passenger capacity was 376. It had advanced safety equipment including safety gauges, fire-fighting pumps, a metal lifeboat and a wooden one, 300 feet of fire hose, thirty buckets for fire fighting, five fire axes, and 76 lifebelts. It was a riverboat, which meant the shoreline would always be in sight on either side.

The boat was 260 feet long and displaced 1,719 tons. By comparison, the Titanic was 882 feet long and displaced 52,310 tons.

The *Sultana* was wooden-hulled, with twin side-wheels powered by high-pressure tubular boilers using two steam engines. The four boilers were each 18 feet long by 46 inches in diameter. They were interconnected; meaning water could travel freely between them. This was partly a safety measure as one of the most dangerous things for a lit boiler to have happen is for all the water to dissipate out as steam. Keeping a constant level of water is critical to safe operation.

The ship departed New Orleans with a problem already apparent: one of the boilers was bulging and leaking. It sailed for two days up the Mississippi with this problem until it reached Vicksburg.

Rather than replace the boiler, which was the correct course of action, the captain ordered a patch to be put on it. The engineer protested initially, insisting that the boiler needed to be replaced. The captain overruled him and the engineer gave in. A local boilermaker told the Captain that extensive repairs were needed and a patch wouldn't last. The Captain insisted he patch the boiler. After initially refusing, the boilermaker placed a patch over the leak. He told the Captain it was a temporary fix and was assured proper repairs would be conducted when the *Sultana* reached St. Louis.

There were two reasons for this, both financial. One, the Captain and other investors were short of funds to pay for a replacement boiler. And two, a boiler replacement would have taken three to four days to accomplish, meaning the *Sultana* would be delayed and lose out on the lucrative business of transporting Union soldiers home, as other steamboats were also heading towards Vicksburg.

A patch was put in place, made of metal thinner than the original boiler wall.

Two days later, the *Sultana* put in at Memphis where another repair job was hastily conducted, but the boiler was not replaced.

Interestingly, the *Sultana* also brought the first word to Vicksburg of President Lincoln's assassination.

Lesson

Greed leads to Speed which Kills.

Speed kills is a theme that has come up in this series again and again. There are many different motivations for people to act in haste; in this case, it was one of the worst: greed.

This was an extreme case of driving with the check engine light on, hoping you can make it. Except a steamship's boilers are bombs, simply waiting to explode. In fact, they are so dangerous that saboteurs used them as bombs during the war. More on that in a bit.

One of the officers of the *Sultana* recalled that as they left Memphis, he'd said: "I'd give all the interest I have in this steamer if we safely land at Cairo."

The interest in the ship was also a contributing cause to the greed: several of the ship's officers and crew had a stake in the ownership of the vessel.

The *Sultana* was sailing up the Mississippi with the crew keeping its fingers crossed that the damaged boiler would hold until they reached their destination.

Cascade Two

Most of the passengers were in poor physical health and unable to deal with a catastrophe.

The majority of the Union soldiers on board were former prisoners of war, coming out of primarily Andersonville and Cahaba. The conditions in their prison, especially those in Andersonville, were horrific. At Andersonville almost 13,000 of the 45,000 prisoners died. As the war ended and the survivors were freed, to get home, the rivers were the best way as the rail system in the south had been largely destroyed. First, though, they had to get to the river. This meant traveling overland. Some were able to ride trains to Jackson, Mississippi. But from there, men already in terrible condition had to walk almost fifty miles to get to Vicksburg.

At Vicksburg, they were housed in camps without tents and with inadequate provisions, making a bad situation worse. This led to the men being desperate to get on board a ship, any ship, and get home. Most of the men were from Ohio, which meant going up the Mississippi to Cairo, Illinois and then onto the Ohio River.

Some of the men were in such bad condition; they had to be carried on board the *Sultana* on stretchers.

Lesson

Physical condition is a factor not only in survival but also in motivation.

These men were understandably very anxious to get home after spending most of the war in a prison camp. However, their condition was so poor that of those who survived the initial explosion and ended up in the water, many either drowned or died of hypothermia, unable to make it to shore.

Cascade Three

The boat was grossly overloaded.

With a legal capacity of 376, it is estimated there were roughly 2,400 people on board the *Sultana*.

While part of the reason was the intense desire for the former POWs to make it back home, the fault lies with the greed of both the ship owners and the Army Quartermaster in charge. We've already seen how the ship captain's rush to make it to Vicksburg prevented him from adequately repairing the boiler. The system was that for each enlisted man he carried he would receive $5 and for every officer $10. And, the captain made an under the table deal with the quartermaster to kick back $1.15 for each soldier carried, an unfortunately rather common practice on the river.

Such was the nature of this scheme that another steamboat already docked at Vicksburg, Lady Gay, received not a single passenger from the Army even though it was larger than the *Sultana* and leaving before her. *Lady Gay* left Vicksburg without a single former POW on board.

Even when another steamboat arrived, the Quartermaster, Reuben Hatch, refused to divvy up the prisoners, insisting they all go on the *Sultana*.

The overcrowding had a direct impact on the explosion of the boilers because it made the boat top-heavy. As it went up the river, every time it took a turn in the Mississippi, the boat would tip. The four boilers were all interconnected and with each tip, water would run out of the high side boilers and into the low side. It's believed that the water level got so low, that the high side would be almost completely drained.

When the water rushed back in to the hot boiler, the one with the patch finally blew, setting off two other boilers.

Lesson

The lure of 'easy' money and a kickback scheme set the stage for disaster. Regulations, concern for safety, common sense all disappeared as the ship's captain and the quartermaster jammed every person they could aboard the *Sultana*, viewing each soul as cash.

The quartermaster clearly violated Army regulations in his greed.

Cascade Four

Traveling up river against the spring flood and the current put more strain on the engines and also made the top-heavy boat more liable to lean when turning.

It was spring and the Mississippi was surging with the run off. The *Sultana* was also going up river, against the current. More steam was required to make way against the force of the water. The Mississippi is a river with many turns and is constantly changing. Indeed, the location of the *Sultana's* wreck today is two miles away from the current course of the Mississippi. Taking each turn in a shallow draft steamboat, grossly overloaded above the waterline ran the risk of the boat capsizing. What didn't seem to factor in to the captain's concerns was if the water level in the boilers ran low and the boat leaned more than normal, the interconnected system between the two sides could cause overheating in the up side boilers and then a reaction as water poured back in as they became down side.

It was while the *Sultana* was navigating among a cluster of islands nicknamed 'Hen and Chickens' that the *Sultana* exploded.

Lesson

Cascade events do just that.

We have the hastily patched boiler, combined with an overloaded boat, combined with extra power needed to travel upriver against the spring surge, combined with a boiler system where water went back and forth from each side of the boat, which was top heavy because it was overloaded and thus was tilting more than was safe.

The Rule of Seven shows how a single event often isn't the cause of a catastrophe. Sometimes it's combining events that don't immediately seem connected, that we find the road to potential disaster.

There is the issue of the boilers themselves. The *Sultana* was less than an hour out from Memphis when the boilers exploded: how could the water level have gotten that low so quickly when the boat topped off so recently?

The design of the boats was to maximize room for passengers and cargo. Space for the engines was secondary. The steam room was small and difficult to work in. Water escaping quickly was not uncommon and sometimes led to explosions. Combine that with one of the *Sultana's* boilers having an inadequate patch on it we see a recipe for the catastrophe.

Cascade Five

Technically, the country was still at war and there is the possibility the explosion was the result of sabotage.

Most people think the Civil War ended on 9 April 1865 when Robert E. Lee surrendered to U.S. Grant at Appomattox Court House.

But the war was not over. Lee had surrendered the Army of Virginia but that was just one of several armies the South fielded. The Government of the Confederacy had not surrendered yet.

President Lincoln was assassinated on 14 April 1865.

Various Southern units surrendered as word of Lee's action reached them. President Johnson announced an end to the insurrection on 9 May 1865, weeks after the *Sultana* explosion. The last Confederate general to surrender did so on 23 June 1865 in the Army of the Trans-Mississippi.

Thus, there is the possibility that a Confederate agent placed a 'coal torpedo' on board the *Sultana* and that was cause of the explosion. One agent, Robert Louden, claimed later that he sabotaged the *Sultana* with just such a device.

An officer in the Confederate Secret Service first conceived the idea of coal torpedoes. They were manufactured in Richmond; right across the street from the famous, Tredegar Iron works. In essence, the equivalent of an artillery shell was made to look like a piece of coal. Actual large pieces of coal were used as casting to make an iron case with a wall about a half-inch thick. The interior was filled with gunpowder. A threaded plug was then put in place. The entire thing was dipped in beeswax and then rolled in coal dust. The final product looked like a lump of coal about four inches to a side and weighing around four pounds.

The torpedo was placed in a coal bin to be loaded onto a steamship. When shoveled into the furnace heating the boilers, it would explode. By itself, the torpedo didn't have enough explosive to sink the ship. However, an explosion right under the boiler, which was pressurized, would lead to that secondary explosion.

Boiler explosions were actually frequent among steamships. Since the ships were made of wood, the subsequent fire would often completely destroy the ship.

The case against Robert Louden has never been made and never will be. A coal torpedo leaves no evidence, looking like a boiler explosion. Louden was a blockade-runner and implicated in other coal torpedo events on the Mississippi. He'd spent a year in a Union prison (which weren't much better than Confederate prisons). He had a brother who was still a prisoner. His father had also been imprisoned. His wife had been arrested. He was a man with more than enough motive for revenge.

The last stop the *Sultana* made, after leaving Memphis, was to load coal at Hopefield, Arkansas, on the other side of the river from Memphis.

One night, while drunk in a bar and later on his deathbed, Louden supposedly admitted the planting a coal torpedo in the *Sultana's* coal.

Lesson

Sabotage is a possibility, but without other cascade events, the death toll would have been much lower.

We'll never know what exactly went wrong with the *Sultana's* boilers. While most dismiss the possibility of a coal torpedo, the fact is they were used and worked. They destroyed other steamboats. In fact, coal torpedoes were so effective, they were used to a long time afterward. OSS and SOE agents in World War II used them. German agents captured on Long Island were carrying coal explosives to use on coal-fired power generating plants.

Cascade Six

The explosion occurred at night, with no other boats in the immediate vicinity to help with rescue.

Things are usually worse at night. The ship departed Memphis at midnight (some fortunate souls who'd gotten off during the brief stop to sample the city's charms didn't make it back in time for sailing). It went across the river, took on coal, and then headed north. The explosion occurred around 2:00 am.

While the *Titanic* went down in the ocean, far from land, the *Sultana* went down in a river, with land tantalizingly close on both sides.

Unfortunately, many of the people on board didn't know how to swim. And most of the former POWs were not in the shape to make a cold water, nighttime, swim to shore. For many who survived the initial explosion, they were faced with a terrible choice: die in the fire that consumed the ship, or jump into the water.

It was April and the water was chilly. Even some who could swim or found wood to float on, succumbed to hypothermia before rescuers could arrive.

The explosion could be seen all the way downriver in Memphis. Several boats immediately cast off to investigate, but they were also battling the same strong flood current. There are reports that a former Confederate in a small boat pulled fifteen soldiers to safety.

Lesson

Catastrophes rarely happen at opportune times.

In Special Forces, it always seemed we were alerted in the middle of the night, often on a weekend. It seems we don't go to war at 9:00 am on Monday morning.

Timing is critical. It affects more than just surviving, it can affect the event itself. Was the chief engineer on duty at 2:00 am?

Studying oil blowouts, it was found that more than half occurred in the hours after midnight, peaking between 2:00 am and 3:00 am. In the Army, the opportune time to attack is before BMNT: Being Morning Nautical Twilight. It's when people are at their least observant.

Almost all the passengers were asleep when the boiler exploded. Anyone who has ever been awoken from sleep into the midst of an explosion can understand the confusion and shock. Hopefully, that's not many of you.

Compounding the fact that many of those on board were former POWs in bad condition, the situation quickly became chaotic. With the loss of the boilers, the ship no longer had any steerage. Flames spread from the area of the boilers, consuming the wooden ship.

Final Event

Three boilers explode. Approximately 1,700 passengers and crew die.

Given all the cascade events, the explosion was almost inevitable. This was case where those in the know—the ship's captain, the engineer—were hoping they could dodge the bullet; have a delusion event occur rather than a catastrophe.

Even if the direct cause was a coal torpedo, the overcrowding led to many unnecessary deaths. The actual catastrophe was horrific, especially for the many former POWs who'd spent years of suffering and now were getting so close the home they'd dreamed of throughout their captivity.

When the boilers blew, lookouts on the *USS Grosbeak* saw the flash of flame miles to the north. The captain of the *Grosbeak* immediately ordered his ship north.

The *Sultana* was shattered by the explosion, which happened amidships. Many passengers crowded onto the deck were blown overboard into the water. Many didn't know how to swim and drowned.

For those clinging to the ship, things were worse as flames consumed the vessel. The exploding boilers spewed burning coal all over the ship. The ship was drifting with the strong current. The passenger deck partially collapsed, sliding passengers into the flames. Then the two smokestacks careened down, smashing people below them.

In the midst of all this, one enterprising soldier bayoneted the 'pet' alligator kept on board the *Sultana* and used its wooden crate as a flotation device.

Ultimately, many initial survivors chose to drown rather than be burned alive. The air was filled with the screams of the dying.

The remains of the *Sultana* eventually ran aground on a small island and then sank.

As dawn broke, the river from the initial explosion down to Memphis was full of bodies, both living and dead. Many of those injured suffered from burns and over 200 died in Memphis hospitals. Bodies were recovered from the river for weeks afterwards.

One small bright spot was the enmity of the war was put aside as Southerners in Memphis did everything they could to help the Union victims of this tragedy.

Lesson

Greed is one of the incubators of tragedy. Whether it's cutting costs or trying to make a profit, when rules are broken, the result is often disaster.

Sadly, this entire event might have been prevented had authorities rightfully removed from power the Quartermaster involved: Reuben Hatch. And, even more tragically, some of the blame for that falls on President Lincoln.

While serving as Quartermaster in Cairo, Illinois, Hatch was arrested for taking bribes while purchasing military supplies. The evidence was damning, but Hatch's brother was the Secretary of State in Illinois and a financial supporter of Abraham Lincoln. Hatch never appeared before a court martial board after his brother wrote Lincoln, asking him to intervene.

Lincoln endorsed a letter proclaiming Hatch's innocence and eventually the case was dropped and Hatch cleared of all charges. Later in the war, while serving in New Orleans in the same position he was given a test on his job as Quartermaster (a position he'd held for almost the entire war). The board found him "totally unfit" for the job. In response, he was reposted to be chief Quartermaster for the Department of the Mississippi and stationed at Vicksburg.

Several officers, including the highest-ranking POW, argued that the *Sultana* was overloaded, but Hatch ignored them.

Ultimately, no one was held responsible in any manner for the *Sultana* disaster.

CATASTROPHE 4:
MULHOLLAND & THE
ST. FRANCIS DAM
Engineering Failure

Quote: During the Los Angeles Coroner's Inquest, William Mulholland said, "this inquest is a very painful for me to have to attend but it is the occasion of that is painful. The only ones I envy about this whole thing are the ones who are dead." In later testimony, after responding to a question, he added, "Whether it is good or bad, don't blame anyone else, you just fasten it on me. If there was an error in human judgment, I was the human, I won't try to fasten it on anyone else." William Mulholland, chief engineer, Water Department Los Angeles

The greatest civil engineering disaster of the 20th Century in the United States has largely been forgotten. It caused the second greatest loss of life in the history of California, second only to the 1906 San Francisco Earthquake. Amazingly, a man who had no traditional training as an engineer designed the dam. Even more interesting, the same man designed the Los Angeles Aqueduct, which just celebrated its centennial in 2013.

THE FACTS

Two and a half minutes before midnight on 12 March 1928, the St. Francis Dam failed, sending a surge of water and debris that killed an estimated six hundred people on its journey to finally pour into the Pacific Ocean.

1877: William Mulholland arrives in Los Angeles

1878: Mulholland begins work as a ditch tender

1886: Mulholland becomes superintendent of Los Angeles Water Company

1908-1913: Mulholland supervises the building of the Los Angeles Aqueduct

1924: Water Wars begin

August 1924: Construction of the St. Francis Dam begins

1926: Dam is completed

1 March 1926: Water begins to fill the reservoir

12 March 1928:
10:30 am: The Dam Keeper notes a new leak. Alerts Mulholland. Mulholland inspects and feels there is no immediate danger

11:57:30 pm: The dam fails

5:30 am: The water finally reaches the Pacific Ocean

THE CASCADING EVENTS

Cascade One

Lack of formal Training and Education.

William Mulholland went from being a ditch digger to the superintendent of the Los Angeles Water Department. Along the way, he gained great practical experience in developing water projects, but never received formal training as an engineer.

Mulholland arrived in Los Angeles in 1877, when the town had a population of only 9,000. He got a job as a *zanjero*, a man who helped maintain the *Zanja Madre*, a large open ditch, which supplied the city with water. Also known as a ditch tender.

Just a few years later, he oversaw the laying of the first iron pipeline in the city. During this time, he studied mathematics, geology, hydraulics and engineering on his own. He was made Superintendent of the Los Angeles Water Department in 1886.

Water is critical for Los Angeles and during Mulholland's time was the limiting factor on the city's growth. In 1908, Mulholland designed and supervised the construction of the Los Angeles Aqueduct. It was a marvel of engineering, completed ahead of time and under budget in 1913. It required only gravity to move water 233 miles from the Owens Valley to Los Angeles. The completion of the aqueduct opened up Los Angeles for a population boom.

There were some who objected to this project. We'll cover that in another cascade event. The key here is that Mulholland was recognized as an engineering genius, despite the lack of formal education and training He was self-taught and learned by experience. He was the first American engineer to utilize hydraulic sluicing to build a dam, and that garnered him national attention and admiration. He consulted on the building of a dam during the construction of the Panama Canal.

In 1914, the University of California at Berkeley gave Mulholland an honorary doctorate. It was inscribed: *'Percussit saxa et duxit flumina ad terram sitientum'* (He broke the rocks and brought the river to the thirsty land).

Lesson

Major endeavors require personnel who are trained and educated, as well as checks and balances on a single person being in charge.

Mulholland grew so powerful and popular that there seemed there was nothing he could not do. At one point, his office was on the top floor of Sid Grauman's theater. He was very close to the Mayor of Los Angeles and was considered a top candidate to run for office (he did say he'd ". . . rather give birth to a porcupine backward" than run for office).

The choice of location for the St. Francis Dam and its design were left entirely in his hands. While his self-education was impressive, the reality was that he learning on the job. While the aqueduct is still in operation, his dams were a different story.

Cascade Two

Bad choice of location, which was suspected but not acted on, and exemption from regulation.

It was while building the aqueduct that Mulholland began to think about building some dams to form reservoirs as a backup source of water. He knew that the aqueduct went through the San Andreas Fault, which meant an earthquake could damage it. Also, the Water Wars (more later) meant there could be an interruption of service.

There was a camp of laborers near the site where he would put the St. Francis dam years later. Mulholland spent time there in 1911 and examined the terrain and geology. He looked at the San Francisquito Canyon because it would be between hydroelectric plants No. 1 and No. 2 when the aqueduct was completed. He felt the topography was suitable since there was a narrowing of the canyon downstream from an area, which could form a large reservoir.

Interestingly, checking the ground, he discovered a mica schist that was severely laminated and faulted. Later it would be determined that this line was part of the San Francisquito Fault. Mulholland had shafts dug to further check the geology.

Years later, when it came time to start building reservoirs, he chose this location. Which is odd, because he'd written about the schist in his 1911 notes. Later geologists said that Mulholland couldn't have known there had been an ancient landslide in the locale where he wanted to put the dam but that the schist should have been a warning sign. The 1911 annual report mentioned San Francisquito Canyon, noting that the rock was rough and threatened slips. Mulholland's chief assistant engineer recalled the schist long after the disaster and noted that they had difficulty 'holding ground' when they put the aqueduct through the area.

The chief electrical engineer for Los Angeles protested the dam site, not for the ground, but because it could only supply power to one of the two power plants nearby. These protests fell on deaf ears since Mulholland had great sway in the city's hierarchy.

Worse, municipalities were exempt from California's dam-safety law, which had been enacted in 1917. This meant when Mulholland chose the site and the design; he was exempt from any external oversight.

We saw in the New London Schoolhouse explosion in the first book how trying to save money can be disastrous. The site for the reservoir was originally to be in Big Tujunga Canyon, further south and closer to Los Angeles than the San Francisquito Canyon.

There were opposing forces at play in order for that to work: first, the property in the Big Tujunga Canyon was priced much higher. Mulholland felt this was almost a holdup of Los Angeles and chose to move further away from the city to the San Francisquito Canyon, where the land could be purchased much more cheaply.

It seems that in doing so, he forgot his report of twelve years earlier indicating potential problems in the area.

Even after the disaster, other engineers were reticent to speak out, even though they had noted the lack of adequate drainage below the dam and the problematic schist. They also noted that Mulholland tended to trust his own judgment far beyond that of anyone else and rarely sought other opinions.

Lesson

Nature does win and it doesn't care. Oversight is needed on large, complex construction problems.

Whether it was the snowstorm that stopped the Donner Party in book one, or the fault line that helped doom the St. Francis Dam, nature takes no side. It just is.

Mulholland can't be blamed for not knowing there had been a landslide in that location so long ago. But his own notes should have given him a moment's pause about the schist. And he should have combined those notes with Cascade Six to consider that he had a big problem on his hands after the dam was built.

While nature doesn't care, we often get into catastrophic situations with it by making poor choices; whether it be the Hastings Cutoff for the Donner Party, or not linking the schist with the seepage of Cascade Six. Nature often gives us warnings, which we ignore at our peril.

Worse, exempting municipalities from a law designed for dam safety, effectively gave free rein to a man like Mulholland. If the law was seen as necessary elsewhere, why wasn't it seen as necessary in all cases?

Cascade Three

A history of failure and ego.

Despite the success of the aqueduct, Mulholland's record wasn't spotless. In 1918 the partial collapse of the Calaveras Dam near San Francisco occurred. Mulholland had supervised the dam's construction and had been considered an expert on the type: an earth fill using the earthen-hydraulic techniques for which Mulholland was known. A portion of the fill upstream fell into the reservoir, requiring reconstruction.

A visiting engineer wrote that Mulholland's work was sloppy and his construction techniques slipshod and crude. More interestingly, the same engineer claimed Mulholland was so conceited that he believed himself immune from criticism.

Lesson

The flip side of burning ambition is the danger of hubris.

Mulholland is a shining example of the American dream of pulling oneself up on one's own merit and hard work. Self-educated, Mulholland taught himself the job; combined with his passion for work, he rose up the ranks to become Superintendent. However, such people can tend to be loners, not team players. When you consider the number of specific experts that would be required to build a major dam today, and then realize that Mulholland not only reconnoitered the dam's location, surveyed it, designed it, and oversaw construction, it's both impressive and scary.

The bottom line is if it works, as in the case of the aqueduct, one is labeled a genius. When it fails, as in the case of the St. Francis Dam, the result is otherwise.

Cascade Four

The Water Wars.

Mulholland was a controversial figure in California even before the St. Francis Dam failed. While building the aqueduct was an engineering success and a boon for Los Angeles, those on the other end of it, the farmers and ranchers in the Owens Valley held a very different perspective.

The acquiring of the water rights in the Owens Valley was divisive, some say underhanded and illegal. Regardless, the result had an impact on the dam built later because of the resulting 'water wars'.

After the aqueduct was finished in 1913, Los Angeles began sucking the Owens Valley dry. By the way, at the opening of the aqueduct, Mulholland made an extremely short speech, five words, which indicates the attitude of Los Angeles toward the water: "There it is. Take it."

By the 1920s, it was becoming difficult for Owens Valley farmers and ranchers to sustain their livelihoods. In 1924, attempts were made to sabotage the aqueduct.

In 1926, Owens Lake was empty.

The pressure of the water wars and the danger that the aqueduct could be destroyed, made Mulholland pursue dams such as the St. Francis with more vigor. He felt the city needed at least a two-year backup supply to the Aqueduct.

After the dam was completed, on 27 May 1927, the Los Angeles Aqueduct was dynamited. This was followed by a second attack, which destroyed another portion, and then more attacks which completely shut down the Aqueduct. This left the St. Francis Dam reservoir as the only northern source of water for the city.

Water was withdrawn and the water level behind the dam fell significantly. After the attacks ceased, the level rose once more, but now problems appeared on the dam. Two fractures appeared on the surface of the dam. Mulholland inspected them, ordered them sealed, and judged they were fixed. As water continued to rise, there were cracks in the abutments along with seepage.

Lesson

Care must be exercised when external factors influence engineering decisions.

The location of the dam was critical. Ultimately, the terrain was a major factor in its failure; thus, even if the design was flawed, the dam might have survived on better footing. The Mulholland Dam, which still stands, is of the same design. However, it was modified after the St. Francis Dam failure.

The Water Wars caused undue stress on the dam early in its life. In a way, the cracks that appeared as the dam was refilled should have been a warning; but Mulholland assumed they were part of the normal operation of the dam.

Cascade Five

The Design was flawed.

The Mulholland Dam was the first such concrete dam built by the Department of Water Works and Supply. Mulholland used much of the same design and stress factors for the St. Francis, even though the St. Francis was on different terrain.

The dam was curved during a time when concrete dams shaped like that were in their infancy. The original design called for it to be built 1,825 feet above sea level, 175 feet above the streambed. The reservoir would have a capacity of 30,000 acre-feet.

Construction began in 1924. Almost immediately, Mulholland began making modifications. Ten feet were added on to the top of the dam, cresting at 1,835 feet above sea level. This apparently small increase required the construction of a 588 feet long wing on the edge of the dam to maintain the height. This also increased the capacity to 38,000 acre-feet. This is a significant increase in capacity and pressure.

While the dam was being built, an engineer who had criticized Mulholland for using faulty cement in the Aqueduct visited the site. He criticized the design, the foundation materials, and the geological conditions. Tests showed that the red conglomerate on which some of the dam rested dissolved when submerged, which is exactly what a dam does. The engineer released a report, which predicted: "This dam, if kept full for any length of time . . . will unquestionably fail." This engineer, Frederick C. Finkle, was considered a premier expert on hydraulic engineering and geology. Such words would have made most men pause, but Mulholland dismissed it as a political ploy, tangential to the Water Wars. Mulholland made no attempt to find a nonpartisan expert to check these issues.

The dam was completed in 1926 and immediately cracks began to appear.

Lesson

Ignoring warnings is a staple of catastrophe.

Mulholland's belief in his own abilities was a blind spot in character that led to tragedy. He designed the Mulholland Dam and then, while it was still being built, transferred those plans to the St. Francis Dam. He was almost experimenting with the plans, having little experience in both the type of dam and the material used. He didn't share his design with other experts to get their feedback and advice. Once more, a project of this magnitude required more than one man to design and build.

Modifications were made during constructions, which meant that even if the original design had been successful, the final product did not adhere to the original. Increasing the plan for the amount of water to be held in the reservoir by over a quarter while the dam was in the process of being built was a move that should have brought some questions from the Water Board, but because of Mulholland's reputation, none dared question him.

Besides Finkle's warning, there was visual evidence of a problem.

Cascade Six

Constant instability wasn't addressed—along with visible evidence of problems.

The dam was completed and water began to fill the reservoir on 12 March 1926. As the water rose, contraction cracks appeared and there was some seepage. Two vertical cracks ran through the height of the dam. Mulholland investigated and announced they were within parameters for a concrete dam of this size. By the following month, the water reached the San Francisquito Fault Line. Seepage began immediately. Mulholland ordered workers to seal the leak, but they couldn't completely stop it and water covered the face of the dam. A pipe was laid from the fault line down to the house of the dam keeper to reroute the water for his personal use.

Concern began to rise about uplift on the dam. Essentially, water goes into the foundation material under pressure. It spreads into the joint between the foundation and the dam material and the pores of the dam itself. The water is trying to move to the downstream side. This water, under pressure, exerts an upward hydraulic pressure known as uplift. Uplift reduces the weight of the dam and thus weakens its force.

A concrete gravity dam collapsed in Pennsylvania in 1911. It killed 78 people and wiped out the community below it. An engineer who reviewed the collapse later consulted with Mulholland, so he must have been aware of the problems associated with uplift. Yet, Mulholland did little to counter uplift at St. Francis.

On 12 March 1928, the dam keeper noted a muddy leak that worried him. So much so, that he called Mulholland. Mulholland and his chief assistant drove out, inspected the dam and the leak, pronounced it safe, and went back to Los Angeles.

The dam keeper and others who lived downstream weren't so sure. Not only was the dam leaking, the ground had seemed soaked for days. People, as they do in the face of uncertainty, joked about it: "See you later if the dam don't break."

Lesson

Sunk cost and we don't see what we don't want to see.

We discussed sunk cost in the Donner Party in book I. This is a slightly different form of it. There comes a time during a long, drawn-out series of cascade events, where one has to accept *sunk cost*, and cut loose from what has already been done in order to stop a catastrophe.

Sunk cost is a past cost that has already been incurred and cannot be recovered. It should not be a factor in current decision-making. The dam had been built, but problems were repeatedly rearing their heads. Mulholland kept trying to literally patch the problems or ignore what even a layman could see about the dam.

Perhaps Mulholland didn't understand what was happening, although he certainly was brilliant enough to grasp the engineering problem. It is more likely he didn't want to see it. Like many disasters, there were warning signs that could have prevented catastrophe. Mulholland literally failed to accept them for what they were, even when called in on the day the catastrophe occurred.

Final Event

The Dam Fails.

Mulholland went back to Los Angeles but the dam keeper could only go back to his house below the dam. And thus became the first casualty when the dam failed at two and a half minutes before midnight on the same day. There were no survivors witnessing the collapse to note the exact moment, but a power drop at the Bureau of Power and Light at that time fixes the time.

A man riding a motorcycle drove past the dam about ten minutes before midnight. He noted nothing out of the ordinary and continued on. About a mile upstream of the dam, he heard a sound over the noise of his motorcycle and stopped. He said it sounded like 'rocks rolling down the mountain.' The sound faded into the distance.

The collapse was sudden and complete. All that was left was a center section, the cover of this book. The rest of the dam broke into smaller pieces, which added to the destruction as they were propelled downstream.

12.4 billions gallons of water headed down the San Francisquito Canyon. One piece of concrete, weighing 10,000 tons was found almost a mile below the dam site, a testament to the power of water.

Most people are unaware of the tremendous power of water. A bathtub holds roughly 40 gallons of water; which weighs 330 pounds. Add in velocity to weight, and you begin to get an idea what destructive power 12.4 billion gallons can bring with it. It's not just the water, it's also the objects the water picks up and carries with it.

The dam keeper, who'd called Mulholland, was among the first to die along with his family. His house was a quarter mile from the dam. When the wall of water hit there, it must have been about 140 feet high. The dam keepers' body, as well as that of his six-year-old son, was never found.

64 workmen at Powerhouse #2 died when the flood hit. It was now 120 feet high and traveling at 18 miles per hour. It turned into the Santa Clara riverbed and began

heading west. 85 men died when a construction camp was swamped when the now 55 foot high wall of water hit, crossing where Interstate 5 now runs. The water followed gravity, along where Route 126 runs.

It wasn't just the water. It was also what the water carried with it: houses, bodies of both people and animals, trees, lumber, parts of bridges; whatever it had torn away.

Finally, after almost five and a half hours, the water reached the Pacific. 54 miles from where the dam had been. Bodies were found in the ocean, washed as far away as Mexico. Many were never found, leaving in doubt the exact number of those killed.

Mulholland was awoken by a phone call, early enough in the disaster, that he was at the dam site by the time the water reached the Pacific. He was a broken man who would never recover.

Lesson

Missing the last chance.

The day the dam failed, Mulholland had one last chance to avoid catastrophe. He heeded the dam keepers' call enough to drive to the dam and inspect it, but he failed to accept the gravity of the situation. He failed to connect it to the other cascade events.

In a way, the dam finally failing is symbolic of cascade events piling up until a catastrophe is inevitable.

Only the middle portion of the dam remained standing, almost a grave marker. That section was dynamited after a boy, climbing up on top, fell to his death when a 'friend' tossed a dead rattlesnake at him as a joke.

Initially some speculated the dam had been sabotaged as a result of the Water Wars.

There was also some degree of urgency to determine the cause of the failure because the Mulholland Dam was built off the same design.

It is only recently that it's been determined that the St. Francis Dam was constructed on the site of an ancient landslide; something that was undetectable at the time to geologists and engineers. But that wasn't the sole cause of the collapse.

At the time it was determined that an error in engineering judgment contributed to the failure, by placing the dam on unstable geologic formations. The dam design also did not handle uplift well with no cutoff walls, a lack of grouting on the bottom and few inspection tunnels with drainage pipes (except for the center of the dam: the only part left standing).

During these investigations, Mulholland, when questioned about using consultants and taking advice admitted: "In general, for the last ten or twelve years, I haven't consulted with anybody, or but very few."

Lesson

Ultimately, it came down one key issue: the construction of such a large and critical structure should not be the sole responsibility of one man, no matter how accomplished.

If others had been consulted, it is very likely that most, if not all the problems would have been discovered. Finkle's assessment should have been paid attention to. At the very least, an outside consultant, who did not have any agenda other than safety, should have been brought in.

A panel was appointed to look at Mulholland Dam. Rather than destroy the dam, it was decided to permanently lower the level of the reservoir behind the dam from 7,900 acre-feet to a maximum of 4,000 acre-feet. A massive amount of earth was emplaced on the downstream side to help against uplift. This had the additional effect, after vegetation was planted, of largely shielding the dam from view.

As a result of this disaster, California passed a new dam safety law in 1929 requiring the State Engineer to review all non-federal dams over 25 feet high or holding more than 50 acre-feet of water. It also allowed the state to employ outside consultants as deemed necessary.

All of that was too late for Mulholland. To his credit, he took full responsibility for the disaster. As noted at the beginning of this section:

During the Los Angeles Coroner's Inquest, William Mulholland said, "this inquest is a very painful for me to have to attend but it is the occasion of that is painful. The only ones I envy about this whole thing are the ones who are dead." In later testimony, after responding to a question, he added, "Whether it is good or bad, don't blame anyone else, you just fasten it on me. If there was an error in human judgment, I was the human, I won't try to fasten it on anyone else." William Mulholland, chief engineer, Water Department Los Angeles

William Mulholland officially resigned in 1929 and died in 1935.

CATASTROPHE 5: THE SINKING OF THE *KURSK*
Poor Training and Maintenance

Quote: "It's dark here to write, but I'll try by touch. It seems like there are no chances, 10%-20%. Let's hope that at least someone will read this. Hello to everyone. There is no need to despair." Captain Lieutenant Dmitri Kolesnikov, commander 7th Compartment (turbine room) Russian submarine Kursk.

THE FACTS

On 12 August 2000, the *Kursk* was taking part in Russian naval exercises in the Barents Sea. When it prepared to fire a dummy torpedo, there was an explosion. Two minutes and fourteen seconds later, there was a second, much larger explosion. After much confusion, lack of communication, and failed rescue attempts, it was finally determined the *Kursk* had gone down with all hands.

December 1994: The *Kursk* is commissioned as the largest attack submarine in the world.

Summer 1999: The *Kursk* conducts its only long-term (6 month) deployment to the Mediterranean to monitor the US Sixth Fleet responding the crisis in Kosovo.

10 August 2000: *Kursk* joins Summer-X fleet exercises, the first large scale naval exercises by the Russian fleet in over ten years.

12 August 2000; 11:28 am: An explosion is registered as the *Kursk* prepares to fire a dummy torpedo during the exercise.

135 seconds later: a second, much greater explosion is registered.

12 August 2000; 6:00 pm: The *Kursk* misses a scheduled transmission.

13 August 2000; 4:50 am: A Russian vessel discovers an anomaly on the bottom.

9 October 2001: Most of the *Kursk* is salvaged.

The Cascading Events

Cascade One

The Russian Fleet was in poor condition and the crew inadequately trained.

With the breakup of the Soviet Union, military funding was drastically cut back. Many of the sailors had gone unpaid for long periods of time. For the Northern Fleet, the majority of submarines had essentially been abandoned, left to rust at their piers. Maintenance on the handful of vessels kept operational was limited. One casualty of the cutbacks was a lack of upkeep on search and rescue equipment.

Kursk was one ship that was kept operational, but only barely. The submarine was said to be unsinkable (déjà vu on that). It was a very large ship, 505 feet long, 78 feet wide, and 59 feet high. It had a double hull, with 11 feet in between the outer and inner hulls, which was designed to sustain damage from a direct torpedo strike. It had 9 watertight compartments along its length.

It was launched in 1994, but the lack of funding kept it tethered to port almost all the time. It conducted only one long deployment, to the Mediterranean in 1999, where it shadowed the American Sixth Fleet. This lack of sea time meant the crew was not sufficiently trained.

When the *Kursk* went to sea in August 2000 to participate in the Summer-X exercise, it was a first for many members of the crew.

Lesson

Training is the baseline of safety, especially for complex systems such as the *Kursk*.

Not only was the crew of the *Kursk* ill-prepared for events, the entire Russian Navy was not ready to deal with a catastrophe.

The lack of training for the crew of the *Kursk* led directly to . . .

Cascade Two

First Explosion.

On the morning of 12 August, the *Kursk* prepared to fire dummy torpedoes at a battle cruiser as part of the exercise. The torpedoes were for training only and contained no warhead. Unfortunately, they were also constructed to a lower standard than regular ones. While the torpedoes had no warhead, they did have a large amount of explosive in terms of the fuel that propelled the torpedo.

After the sub was raised, the instructions for loading practice torpedoes were recovered. Except they were for a different model of torpedo and were missing some key steps for the process. The crew had never been tested for their readiness for firing the practice torpedoes. An event they'd never done before.

The cause of this first explosion was finally ascribed to high-test peroxide (HTP) leaking from a faulty weld in a torpedo's casing. This first explosion destroyed the torpedo room, killing everyone in the front compartment.

Despite being waterproof, the sections were not blast proof. The explosion moved rearward through air-conditioning vents. The command post was in the second compartment and all 36 men there were most likely killed in the initial explosion. If not killed, they were definitely incapacitated.

Lesson

Inadequate training and subpar construction are a perfect combination for catastrophe.

One thing we learned in Special Forces was that training exercises were often as dangerous as combat. Conducting high-risk training requires detailed planning and preparation. The fact the crew was firing these torpedoes for the first time and didn't even have the right manual for them is a glaring error.

The detonation of the first torpedo ignited a blaze the raised the temperature of the first compartment to almost five thousand degrees Fahrenheit. This caused . . .

Cascade Three

Second Explosion.

It's possible the *Kursk* might have survived the first explosion. It still had watertight compartments and power, although it had settled to the ocean bottom since no one in the command section was active. But two minutes and fourteen seconds after the first explosion, the heat caused five to seven other torpedoes to explode.

This explosion was 250 times more powerful than the first, as the *Kursk* was carrying a combat load of live torpedoes in addition to the training ones. The explosion was so strong it registered on seismographs in Europe as a 4.2 on the Richter scale. It was detected around the world as far away as Alaska.

Lesson

In a contained system, an initial failure almost always gets worse.

Despite taking to sea for wargames, the *Kursk* carried a full complement of ordnance. This is not atypical, but it certainly heightened the dangers in any operation. The presence of torpedoes with warheads doomed the ship.

Cascade Four

Too long to recognize there was a problem.

Out of sight, out of mind applies to an extent here. While the effect of the dual explosions was picked up, the Russian fleet at first did not realize the *Kursk* was in trouble. Although the double explosions decimated the ship, twenty-three of the crew survived those blasts and gathered in a rear, waterproof compartment.

The surface ships nearby detected the explosions, but it was considered part of the exercise. Some of the reports of underwater explosions were simply ignored. It wasn't until the *Kursk* missed a scheduled contact late in the day that Russian officers became concerned; this was six hours after the explosions. One of tenets of rescue operations is that speed is of the essence.

It took the Russian Navy sixteen hours to locate the *Kursk* resting on the bottom. It took another fifteen hours to send down the first rescue vehicle, a total thirty-one hours.

Interestingly, the U.S. Security Adviser and Secretary of Defense were informed by American intelligence agencies that the *Kursk* had sunk even before the Kremlin.

The first rescue submersible collided with the *Kursk* and was damaged. The second one, made operational by salvaging parts off the first one, got the incorrect heading and missed the ship.

Various countries, including the United State and Britain, offered assistance, but were turned down by the Russians.

There were reports of SOSs being tapped out from the *Kursk*, but they were never officially acknowledged.

Lesson

While speed often causes catastrophes, after one occurs, it is of the essence.

One can ascribe the failure to acknowledge the sinking of the *Kursk* to a number of factors:

1. Inexperience in the fleet in recognizing the sounds heard over sonar. American analysts immediately knew that the submarine had experienced explosions, but the Russians were uncertain.

2. The *Kursk* was considered unsinkable. Officers were reluctant to go to a negative conclusion in the absence of clear evidence in the form of wreckage.

3. The Russian system weighed heavily in favor of not passing bad news up the chain of command. The commander of the Northern Fleet, once he was finally informed, was loath to pass the news on to the Kremlin. There were two informal rules left over from the Soviet system: don't take responsibility for failure; and don't send bad news to the Kremlin. In a future book, we'll see how this played in to the Chernobyl disaster. This lack also caused another problem: Putin was vacationing at the time and since he wasn't told the severity of the incident, he was video taped smiling and enjoying himself. This caused a severe public outcry once the truth got out as most Russians believe Putin had known. This caused Putin to clamp down on the press in order to avoid a similar PR nightmare; a policy that has continued through his reign.

4. The commander also had a practical reason: there wasn't much he, or the rest of the Russian Navy could do. The cutbacks had gutted the capability of the Navy to conduct a rescue, which leads to . . .

Cascade Five

Rescue gear was inadequate.

The *Kursk* was equipped with a rescue buoy, which should have deployed right away at the first explosion. It was located near the rear on top of compartment seven. It was supposed to float to the surface and transmit an emergency signal helping rescuers locate the vessel. There are several versions why it didn't deploy. There are reports it had repeatedly malfunctioned and it was welded into place. Another report was that when the *Kursk* did its one deployment to the Mediterranean to observe the American fleet, officers were worried it would accidently deploy and reveal their location so they had it disabled.

If either of these is true, they contributed to the failure to realize the *Kursk* had sunk and the failure to locate it in a timely manner.

The fleet's rescue ship was a converted lumber carrier and hopelessly out of date and in poor shape. The two submarines to be used in a possible rescue were also in poor shape, with the Russian eventually having to cannibalize one to get the other functional.

The Russians had practically no experience in an underwater rescue operations. Even when they finally accepted foreign help, they could provide little assistance. When Norwegian divers tried to open a hatch, the Russians told them that they had to open it counterclockwise or else they would break it. Frustrated when that didn't work, the Norwegians finally ignored the 'advice', turned it the other way, and opened it.

Lesson

Rescue equipment is often a last priority; until a catastrophe strikes, when it's too late.

Part of a delusion mindset is to ignore rescue equipment and training, since many believe it leads to a negative mindset. Often rescue gear is in place, but no one knows how to use it. More often, the gear is inadequate to the task. We saw in book one that the *Titanic* had enough lifeboats for only 52% of those on board. The Russian navy did not have the equipment that could have saved the twenty-three survivors. We know twenty-three survived the initial explosions and sinking, because a note (quoted from at the beginning of this event) was recovered from one of the survivors.

Cascade Six

A cover up hampered rescue and salvage operations and also obscured lessons learned from the death of the sailors.

For a long time the Russian Navy claimed the *Kursk* was sunk after colliding with another submarine, most specifically the *USS Memphis*. The point was that the sinking was not the Navy's fault, but the United States. This façade was maintained until the bulk of the vessel was finally raised and the damage could be inspected.

Lesson

Failure to learn the gift of failure.

Often authorities focus too much on damage control to their careers rather than real damage control. Blame is often shifted, distracting from learning the real causes and problems and insuring that a similar catastrophe could happen, since the real problems are never addressed.

Final Event

Every member of the crew died.

No one knows exactly how long the survivors in the ninth compartment lived. Examining the wreckage after it was brought up, it was determined that a cartridge for a chemical oxygen generator (a piece of survival gear designed to release oxygen in emergencies) came in contact with seawater as the compartment was filled to the waist at this time. This caused a chemical reaction. A flash fire burned through the compartment. Even then, some of the men survived by diving under the water.

Unfortunately for them, the fire consumed all the oxygen left in the compartment.

When a Dutch company was awarded a contract to raise the *Kursk*, their first concern was exactly the same factor that had sunk the ship: an explosion from torpedoes still in the bow. So, they cut the bow off from the rest of the submarine using a long tungsten carbide cable.

The rest of the ship was brought up and put on a barge for examination. Finally, answers to the questions of what had happened were finally learned.

The long held excuse that a United States submarine had collided with the *Kursk* was discredited.

A Russian admiral released a top-secret report summarizing the incident and claiming it was the result of: "stunning breaches of discipline, shoddy, obsolete and poorly maintained equipment . . ." and "negligence, incompetence and mismanagement."

He concluded that what happened inside the submarine "was hell."

CATASTROPHE 6:
PEARL HARBOR

"Should hostilities once break out between Japan and the United States, it would not be enough that we take Guam and the Philippines, nor even Hawaii and San Francisco. To make victory certain, we would have to march into Washington and dictate the terms of peace in the White

House. I wonder if our politicians (who speak so lightly of a Japanese-American war) have confidence as to the final outcome and are prepared to make the necessary sacrifices." Admiral Yamamoto, Commander Japanese Navy. (Note that this quote was used extensively for propaganda purposes by the United States by leaving out the last sentence)

The attack on Pearl Harbor was a catastrophe for both the attackers and those attacked. While a tactical victory for the Japanese, it ultimately led to a strategic defeat. Thus, we have to look at the cascade events for Pearl Harbor from both sides, seeing how they played against each other and why it turned out badly for both parties.

What the Japanese hoped would be a 'knockout blow' against the United States turned out to be something very different. And the pride of the US Navy was savaged in an attack that had a result beyond the worst nightmares of most military planners.

In this catastrophe, we have to do a action-reaction series of cascade events, with both sides making the events of 7 December 1941 almost inevitable. And we have to look at strategic (big picture) and tactical events.

THE FACTS

At 7:55 am, local time, the Japanese begin an aerial assault on Pearl Harbor and other military targets (airfields) on Oahu in the Hawaiian Islands.

After an assault of 2 hours and 20 minutes, the attack is over. Eighteen ships are sunk, 2,400 Americans are killed, and 1,200 are wounded. Over 300 aircraft are destroyed.

9 February 1904: Japanese destroyers launch a surprise attack on the Russian Far East Fleet at Port Arthur, crippling the Russians. They had not been at war. They were now.

July 1937: Japan invades China.

December 1937: On the Yangtze River evacuating US Personnel from Nanking, the *USS Panay* is sunk by Japanese aircraft. Japan claims it was an accident and pays reparations.

July 1940: The United States imposes an embargo and sanction on Japan, directed at stopping their expansion in Asia.

January 1941: Admiral Yamamoto proposes an attack on Pearl Harbor to other officers.

16 November 1941: The first vessels, submarines, depart Japan heading toward Hawaii.

26 November 1941: The main Japanese fleet departs Japan for Hawaii.

7 Dec 1941: The Japanese attack Pearl Harbor and other military targets in Hawaii.

BOB MAYER

8 December 1941: President Roosevelt asks Congress for a declaration of war against Japan. The United States enters World War II.

The Map

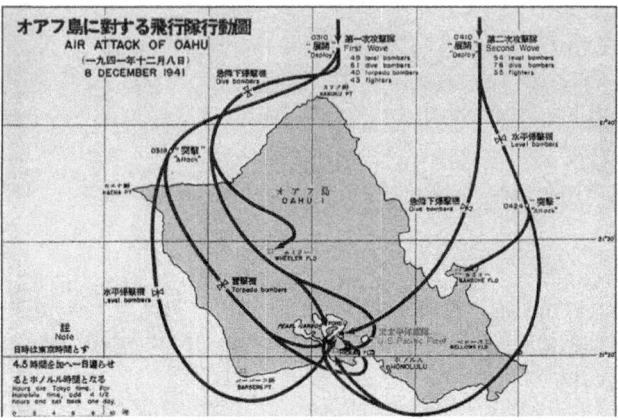

The Cascading Events

Cascade One

Political misunderstanding and maneuvers that backfired.

Fueled by Nationalistic goals, the Japanese begin to build an empire in the west Pacific. The Japanese begin to expand their land base and solve its raw material supply dilemma by invading other countries and bringing its import market under its own control. The primary one of concern was China. The Japanese invaded northern China via Manchuria in July 1937.

In response, the United States began economic sanctions against Japan. These escalated to trade embargoes. The goal was to force the Japanese to withdraw. Psychologically, though, these had the exact opposite effect, causing the Japanese to expand further.

When the United States, then an exporter of oil, embargoed that commodity in July 1941, the Japanese felt their hand had been forced.

Lesson

Carl Von Clausewitz is famous for saying the "War is the continuation of *politik* by other means."

The manner in which Japanese and American politicians misjudged each other is matched only by the way Japanese and American military officers misjudged each other.

To perhaps over simplify things, economic sanctions appear an excellent solution in theory, but end up usually hurting both national pride and the citizenry. In this case, the oil embargo particularly inflamed the Japanese military because oil is essential to military operations: ships, planes, tanks, and trucks all run on oil.

On top of this, the Soviet-Japanese Neutrality Pact signed on 13 April 1941, removed a threat to Japan (and vice versa to Russia), allowing Japan to concentrate on the Pacific Theater.

It was obvious to both the United States and Japan they were on a collision course for war. The sinking of the *Panay* on the Yangtze in 1937 inflamed the American public. While political leaders on both sides continued to talk of desiring peace, the military planned for war.

Cascade Two

Military strategic planners in both countries seriously miscalculated each other.

Having spent many years in the military, I have an idea how military planning works. War Plans are developed based on possible scenarios. We had large safes in a secure room with all the war plans for every single A-Team in our Group. These were extremely detailed plans down to drop zones, hide sites, etc. etc. In the 1930s, as tensions escalated between the two countries, staffs drew up plans to counter the other. However, plans are based on estimate of enemy capabilities and possible actions. In a way, each staff plans against the plan they think the other side has.

In both cases, some very serious mistakes were made.

As a result of the U.S. oil embargo, rather than submit, the Japanese decided to seize the Dutch East Indies and its oil supply. With the war raging in Europe, the Japanese felt the various colonial territories were ripe for the picking except for one problem: the American fleet.

The Japanese believed they needed six months for conquer the East Indies, and therefore needed six months of freedom from the American Navy. Except the American Navy had no plan to interfere. In fact, War Plan Orange, initially drawn up in 1911, called for withholding supplies and reinforcements from west Pacific outposts, primarily the Philippines, and building up Naval Power until a sufficient force could set sail and engage the Japanese in a decisive surface battle.

This plan, by the way, was based on the theories of Alfred Thayer Mahan, a Naval Academy graduate from the class of 1859. Thayer very much believed, unlike Custer, in the concentration of force. He did not believe that the fleet should piecemealed out. Mahan's writings on Naval strategy were so popular they were required reading not only in the United States Navy, but also that of Germany and Japan. As a sidebar, he also is credited with coming up with the term 'Middle East' for that part of the world.

As an update to Plan Orange, which focused on the defense until a powerful fleet could set sail (at least six months and some believed two years), Admiral Stark, Chief of Naval Operations, signed Plan Dog, which outlined a defensive war in the Pacific while the focus was on defeating the Germans in Europe. The Navy's goal in the Pacific was to keep the Japanese out of the eastern Pacific and keep supply lines to Australia open. With the blessing of President Roosevelt, Stark also ordered the Pacific Fleet to deploy forward from San Diego to Pearl Harbor. The commander of the Pacific Fleet objected so strongly to this, he was replaced.

U.S. war planners assumed that the Japanese would attack the Philippines. Few believed or even conceived that the Japanese would attempt the long-range strike (4,000 miles), at Pearl Harbor. They believed this not only because the Philippines were closer to Japan, but also because U.S. forces stationed there would threaten Japanese lines of communication and supply. No one thought the Japanese had the forces to attack *both*.

What American planners didn't focus on was the last time Japan took on a major power: in 1904 the Japanese launched a surprise attack on the Russian Fleet at Port Arthur, sinking two battleships and a cruiser. As you can see elsewhere in this book, this attack was part of the destruction of the Russian Navy and a cascade event for the Russian Revolution and the fall of Czar Alexander.

On the Japanese side, Admiral Yamamoto, while planning for the Pearl Harbor attack, prophesized: "I shall run wild considerably for the first months or a year, but I have utterly no confidence for the second and third years."

Lesson

Strategic plans based on false assumptions can lead to disaster.

In book one in this series discussing Custer, I discussed how militaries are always planning to fight the last war. Even in war planning, we often look back for lessons learned, always a smart move, and apply them to our plans. However, sometimes this ignores changes, particularly technological ones.

Yamamoto was proved correct as the war in the Pacific changed six months later at the Battle of Midway. This had to do not only with strategic issues, but a key tactical mistake the Japanese made by focusing on battleships. The aircraft carrier did not exist when Mahan was coming up with his theories. Also, submarine warfare was in its infancy. The focus on the battleship by almost every country going into World War II would prove to be so misplaced, that there is not a single battleship deployed in the world any more.

Bottom line:

The United States was wrong in believing that the Philippines would be the primary target (the Philippines *were* attacked after Pearl Harbor and still weren't prepared!) and Pearl Harbor was safe from attack.

The Japanese were wrong in believing that the United States would immediately respond to their expansion in the far east.

Cascade Three

Warnings were ignored and/or not given to those who needed to get the warnings.

Once more, this happened on both sides with dire consequences.

On 27 January 1941, 10 months before the actual attack on Pearl Harbor, the Ambassador to Japan wired Washington that he'd discovered the Japanese were planning a surprise attack on Pearl Harbor. This is right after Yamamoto proposed the concept.

He wasn't believed. The Philippines would be the object of a Japanese attack, not Pearl Harbor.

Some have said that U.S. cryptoanalysis had broken the Japanese Code and deciphered messages about the pending attack on Pearl Harbor. Further research, though, reveals that this might not be true. A project named Magic worked on breaking down Japanese diplomatic codes and had great success until the Japanese went to a machine generated code, much like the German Enigma. No one will ever really know the truth about because even if the code had been broken early enough, the government had to keep this secret in order to have the Japanese keep using the code. One only needs to look at the Coventry bombing to see the horrible Catch-22 of covert operations.

However, U.S. intelligence services were reading a lot of the low-level traffic. The information however, was rarely disseminated to those who might be able to use it.

At least one person on the other side, Admiral Nomura, the Naval Councilor on the Supreme War Council, reported that the Americans were reading his message traffic.

He was not believed. Curiously, Nomura became the Japanese ambassador to the United States in 1940 and actually pushed for a conciliation between the two countries. His entreaties to his own government were rejected.

The bottom line was that there were enough messages, warnings, and far-sighted people on both sides to realize something was about to happen.

Lesson

Enough red flags were raised that while it was believed war was inevitable, the exact way the war would start was uncertain.

Of course, it is easy in retrospect to cherry pick certain warnings. We have to accept there were probably numerous other warnings of potential events that never played out.

Going with the concept of the 10th Man from the end of this book, the possibility of an attack on Pearl Harbor should have been given serious consideration. Both the Army and the Navy commanders in Hawaii were relieved of command after the attack. Each needed an officer on their staff working on possibilities beyond those expected to unfurl in War Plan Orange; especially if the Japanese didn't operate according to script.

Cascade Four

Tactical considerations worked both ways.

The Japanese also followed Mahan's teachings. Their goal for the attack was to cripple the American Pacific Fleet. To that end, they focused on sinking the ships of the line: battleships. What's odd about this, is that they planned on doing it with their aircraft carriers, not their own battleships.

Thus while they saw the power of the airborne assault on ships, they didn't see their own vulnerability to it. If they had, they would have focused more on destroying the American aircraft carriers, which weren't present in Pearl Harbor on the day of the attack.

Due to operational and maintenance requirements, no carrier was present on December 7th. The *Enterprise* had just delivered planes to Wake Island and was returning. On Sunday morning it, and its Task Force, was 215 miles west of Oahu. Interestingly, the Japanese chose to approach Hawaii from the north, otherwise there is a chance the *Enterprise* might have spotted the enemy fleet.

Lexington was en route to Midway Island to deliver aircraft. On Sunday morning it, and its Task Force, was 500 miles southeast of Midway.

Saratoga had just completed overhaul at Puget Sound Navy Yard and was arriving in San Diego to pick up her air group before departing for Pearl Harbor.

Yorktown and *Wasp* were in the Atlantic. The *Hornet* was carrying out her shakedown cruise.

Thus even though the bulk of the American fleet lay in ruin on the evening of December 7th, the ships that would turn the tide of the war within a year were all unscathed.

On the American side, a serious tactical miscalculation was that the anchorage at Pearl Harbor was too shallow for a torpedo attack from the air to work. With current technology, this was correct. An airdropped torpedo tended to hit the water nose first (due to the weight of the warhead), plunge down to around 45 feet, then level out, and rise up to running depth of 13 to 20 feet below the surface.

Pearly Harbor is roughly 30 feet deep except in shipping channels, which go down to 45 feet. Thus, the Navy felt confident that this danger wasn't something to consider. However, this ignored the fact that the British Royal Navy had modified some of their torpedoes and attacked Italian harbors as shallow as 24 feet. While the Navy Department had this information five months before Pearl Harbor was attacked, they never forwarded it to Admiral Kimmel at Pearl Harbor.

Torpedoes did the majority of damage to ships in the harbor on December 7th.

However, there is a flip side to this that the Japanese didn't fully comprehend. They 'sank' eight battleships, but because the ships went down in the relatively shallow water, six of them were returned to service. Only the *Arizona* and the *Oklahoma* were complete losses.

Aircraft were a secondary target. Even with all the fear of war, the greater fear was sabotage. Thus, aircraft were parked wingtip to wingtip so they could be guarded more easily. Which made them perfect targets for Japanese aircraft. The navy had 92 aircraft destroyed and 31 damaged. The army had 77 destroyed and 128 damaged.

On the negative side for the Japanese, their focus on destroying battleships and aircraft meant they didn't make the island's infrastructure a priority. This is understandable because the objective of the attack was a short-term gain. In terms of a long war, though, not destroying port facilities, fuel storage depots, docks and shipyards meant that the port could be back in action relatively quickly. Not only back in action, but able to repair much of the damage caused to the ships in a surprisingly short amount of time.

Lesson

Tactical plans need to be made for the most likely threat and then be updated as technology changes.

Everyone had acceptable reasons for making the decisions they did and subsequent actions. Hindsight allows us to see the errors. But this also allows us to see the type of thinking that led to poor tactical decisions.

In some cases, it was lack of information: the fact the British had conducted successful torpedo attacks in shallow water was one such piece of information.

In others it was lack of point of view: the fact the Japanese were counting on their carriers to carry off this daring plan to destroy battleships, should have made them realize that carriers were going to be pre-eminent in the coming war. If they had sunk even just the *Enterprise* and the *Lexington*, it would have changed the course of the war significantly, as both played key roles seven months later at the Battles of the Coral Sea and *Enterprise* at Midway. (Curiously, the *Lexington* and her sister ship, *Saratoga*, had conducted naval exercises employing surprise attacks on Pearl Harbor before the war: successfully).

The Japanese focus on short-term tactical gain to the detriment of long term strategic gain was evident not just in the lack of infrastructure destruction but also in the attack itself.

Cascade Five

New technology was not used correctly.

While the shallow torpedo was new technology and used effectively by the Japanese, the Americans had a piece of technology that, while it worked properly, was not utilized correctly: radar.

Radar is coined from the term 'radio detection and ranging' and in 1941, a number of countries were experimenting with it. Not only was the United States working on radar, the Army and the Navy were working on it separately, not necessarily a good thing.

The Navy put its first working system, which could detect planes up to one hundred miles, in the battleship *New York* in 1939. It was tested and more systems were ordered. One was placed in the USS *California*, which, on December 7th, was anchored at Pearl Harbor.

With its radar off.

The *California* was one of the battleships sunk.

The Army developed two systems, one mobile and one fixed. They deployed the first six mobile radar sets to Oahu, indicating someone thought the island might need early warning against aircraft. They were spaced around the island, with one on the north end, set in a mountain range at an altitude of 532 above sea level with a clear view of the ocean at Opana Point.

At 7:02 on December 7th, the two privates operating the set picked up a flight of aircraft 136 miles due north. First, it's amazing the set worked that well. Second, as anyone who has served will tell, it's great that two privates in an isolated post like that, were standing to their task so diligently. They called it in to the "Intercept Center." They'd never seen a target reading so large and since they were still in training, they failed to rely that information.

A lieutenant took the report and assumed it was a flight of six B-17 bombers that were due in from the mainland, landing to rest and refuel, en route to the Philippines. The vector on which the target was approaching was almost exactly the route the B-17s would be on. He didn't pass the warning on.

Lesson

Having safety and alert protocols and equipment in place are only useful if they are used.

If the radar reading had been interpreted correctly and acted on appropriately, the military would have had 50 minutes to react. Not much time, but enough that at least the sailors on the ships in Pearl Harbor would have stood to and many not caught in their bunks as bombs fell. Some of the ships might have been able to get underway, although that had a negative possibility if one of them was sunk the channel (the *Nevada*, after getting underway and struck again, was beached to prevent such a thing happening) or got out of the harbor into deeper water and sank.

Cascade Six

Timing is everything.

Much like the Sultana explosion occurred in the middle of the night, Pearl Harbor occurred at the worst time of the week for a peacetime military unit: Sunday morning. The slowest time on any military post whether it be Army, Navy or Air Force, is Sunday morning. Many soldier and sailors were resting after a night on the town.

In any organization or technology there is a time when things are most vulnerable. It is normally the time when the people using the technology or in the organization are the most relaxed.

For the military, an axiom is to always be prepared at the time the enemy expects you to be least prepared.

Looking at some of the catastrophes covered in these first two books, let's check the timing of the Final Event:

Pearl Harbor: 7:52 am on a Sunday morning.

Titanic: 11:40 pm to 2:20 am

Sultana: 2:00 am

Texas Schoolhouse Explosion: scant minutes before school let out

Lesson

Bad things rarely happen at opportune times.

Final Event

At 7:48 am on December 7th, 1941, the Japanese Empire conducted a surprise assault on the island of Oahu, primarily focused on the American Pacific Fleet in the harbor, with a secondary objective of destroying military aircraft at outlying bases.

The final tally was:
Navy: 2,009 KIA; 710 wounded.
Army: 218 KIA; 364 wounded.
Marines: 109 KIA; 69 wounded.
Civilians: 68 killed; 35 wounded.

Aircraft:
Navy: 92 destroyed; 31 damaged.
Army Air Corps (there was no separate Air Force branch at the time): 77 destroyed; 128 damaged.

Ships:
Battleships: 2 destroyed; 6 damaged.
Cruisers: 0 destroyed; 3 damaged.
Destroyers: 0 destroyed, 3 damaged.
Auxiliaries: 1 destroyed, 4 damaged.

The United States came back from the devastation of the Pearl Harbor attack even faster than Admiral Yamamoto had feared. At the Battle of the Coral Sea, 7-8 May 1942, the Navy stopped the Japanese from advancing (although the *Lexington* was sunk). On at the Battle of Midway, 4-7 June 1942, the U.S. Navy delivered a devastating blow, sinking four Japanese carriers and turning the tide of the war.

Lesson

The attack had mixed results, but not for those killed or injured. Either side might have avoided a catastrophe if they had focused more on the reality of the situation and not the assumptions each made about the other.

While the United States made numerous misjudgments and mistakes, the larger failure falls upon Japanese shoulders in the long term. Not only did the U.S. military recover quickly, but also the emotional response of Americans to a 'sneak attack' galvanized the country and unleashed a powerful force that would crush Japan in less than four years.

When thinking about the CARVER formula from the end of the book, remember that the E stands for Effect. For every action we take, we must consider the long-term effect.

CATASTROPHE 7: ALIVE! URUGUAYAN AIR FORCE FLIGHT 571

Perseverance Triumphs Over Tragedy

"It was repugnant. Through the eyes of our civilized society it was a disgusting decision. My dignity was on the floor having to grab a piece of my dead friend and eat it in order to survive. But then I thought of my mother and wanted to do my best to get back to see her. I swallowed a piece and it was a huge step - after which nothing happened." Dr. Robert Canessa

This disaster, while tragic, contains some of the most inspiring stories of survival and courage you will ever encounter. In the face of overwhelming odds, a handful of people survived a plane crash, freezing temperatures, high altitude, an avalanche and a rescue being abandoned and then two of them made an almost impossible trek across the Andes to get rescue.

This story is almost the inverse of the Donner Party from the first book in this series. It is a story that shows what the human spirit is capable of.

THE FACTS

On 13 October 1972, Uruguayan Flight 571, carrying 45 passengers and crew, crashed in the Andes. 12 died in the crash and five the day after and another on the 8th day. An avalanche swept over the crash site on the 29th of October, killing another 8. Starving, the survivors turned to feeding on their dead. Two members made a ten-day trek across the mountains and finally made contact, bringing a rescue.

13 October 1972. Uruguayan Flight 571 carrying a rugby team and friends and family, takes off from Montevideo en

route to Santiago, Chile with 40 passengers and 5 crew on board. In thick cloud cover the plane crashes. 5 dead and 7 missing.

14 October: Five more people die of their injuries.

21 October: Another dies. They hear over a transistor radio that the search for them has been called off.

22 October: The decision is made to eat the dead.

24 October: 6 of the missing are found, dead.

29 October: An avalanche sweeps over the crash site, killing 8.

17 November: They discover the tail section of the plane, which has batteries.

24 November: They return to the tail section with the radio, but are unable to transmit.

12 December: Three set out to the west to get help. One is forced to turn back.

20 December: The two make contact with a rancher.

22 December: First rescue mission and takes out six people.

23 December: Second rescue mission takes out the remaining eight.

26 December: A newspaper reports the cannibalism.

28 December: The survivors give a press conference describing their ordeal.

THE CASCADING EVENTS

Cascade One

Bad weather and navigational errors.

Bad weather caused a delay in the flight and then influenced the pilot to choose a longer flight path. Both turned out to be fatal decisions.

Originally, the plane departed on the 12th of October, but poor weather caused it to stop in Mendoza, Argentina. The next day, it was decided because of a combination of poor weather and the plane's limited ceiling to take a circuitous route. First they would fly south, along the eastern front range of the Andes, then turn west and head for a low pass through the mountain range, and then turn north on the western side of the mountains to descend to Santiago.

This was before the days of GPS, when pilots often relied on dead reckoning. There's a reason it's called *dead* reckoning. In essence, the crew worked off their speed and time in flight, since clouds prevented them from using landmarks. After what was felt sufficient time had passed, the pilot radioed Santiago that he was over Curico, Chile and ready to descend.

Unfortunately, the pilot had failed to take into account a strong headwind. The plane was not as far west as he thought. Still in the mountains, the plane was doomed. The only positive aspect was that it didn't smash headlong into a mountainside.

LESSON: Simple errors can have dire consequences.

The pilot's miscalculation of the dead reckoning, failing to take into account a strong headwind, indicates error at a fundamental level. Dead reckoning is actually a more complex art than simply calculating speed by time. Air density is also a factor. Headwind is a basic factor.

There are numerous examples throughout history where dead reckoning produced erroneous results. Ships have to factor in things like ocean current to the their speed and time.

The Andes are the highest mountain range in South America, making them a formidable obstacle. Antoine de Saint-Exupery, the author of The Little Prince, flew the Andes back in the late 1920s and knew the dangers of navigating through the mountains.

Despite the time pressure, with the weather that bad, the pilot might well have delayed the flight another day. One of the most difficult decisions for a pilot to make is to delay takeoff. No one is happy with that decision but it can save lives.

Cascade Two

The plane crashes.

At 13,800 feet the plane clipped a mountain, ripping off the right wing. The wing flew back and cut off the stabilizer. Immediately afterward, another mountain took off the left wing. What remained was essentially a fuselage hurtling through the air. A propeller blade sliced through the cabin as its wing was torn off. The tail section of the plane ripped away.

The fuselage slammed into the snow-covered ground on a downslope, a most fortunate angle, and slid down before coming to rest in a snow bank.

In a way, the survivors were extraordinarily lucky to live through the crash. The loss of the wings but not an impact with the cabin; the downslope; the snow; all combined to allow most of those on board to live.

Lesson

Good luck sometimes is mixed with bad luck.

Any time someone survives a plane crash, they are flushed relief. Except the plane crash is usually only just the first of many problems. There have been reports of passengers surviving a crash on a runway, and sitting there stunned and unmoving as jet fuel ran down the aisle and exploded, negating the crash survival.

In Special Forces, an airborne infiltration, while adrenaline producing and exciting, had to be put into context as simply the first step in the mission: the means of getting us there.

Compounding the situation though, was that the pilot had radioed in the wrong position. This had a negative effect two ways: search and rescue went to the wrong area; and the co-pilot told the survivors, before he died, that he though they were on the west side of the Andes.

After eleven days, the situation turned even bleaker when they heard over a small transistor radio they had, that the search for them had been called off.

As most of the survivors had their spirits shattered by this news, one of them called out to the others: "Hey, boys! There's some good news. We just heard on the radio. They've called off the search."

Crazy, right? That's what the others thought, demanding why he thought it was good news.

"Because it means that we're going to get out of here on our own," was the reply.

That was a rallying point for a group that had sunk as low as it could go. Every team needs a person like that, someone who can see the opportunity in even the worst moment. Who can bolster spirits when they've frayed to the breaking point.

Cascade Three

Resorting to cannibalism.

Unlike the Donner Party, where resorting to cannibalism was the result of numerous bad choices, here it was part of series of necessary choices.

As I discuss under airplane crashes in *The Green Beret Survival Guide*, the rule is to stay near the wreckage as it provides both resources and is also the easiest thing for searchers to find (especially in these days of transponder beacons). In the movie *Into The Gray* it made absolutely no sense for those survivors to head off into the wilderness. For the sake of "entertainment" the writers of that movie simply ignored the fact the plane had a transponder, and that any such flight would be missed and searchers sent out.

But this situation was different. There was no transponder. The plane was resting on snow, at high altitude, and was, as cruel fate would have it, painted white on top. Almost two weeks had passed and they knew the search had been ended.

Still, though, the group waited, against hope, that someone might find them. They weren't certain where they were (although they were working off the co-pilot's wrong report on their location, which led to the crash in the first place).

Running out of supplies, the group made the extreme decision to turn to anthropophagy, which is a nice way of saying cannibalism. This decision was not made lightly. Have you ever considered being in such a situation? Where it was make this choice or die? What would you do?

We also need to remember that they were at high altitude, in the freezing cold, where the body burns more energy. The survivors held a meeting and made this most difficult decision. Canessa, whose quote opened this section was the one who took the initiative. There were some who refused to partake. One died not long afterward.

Cascade Four

An avalanche strikes the party.

Sixteen days after the crash, an avalanche swept over the plane, killing eight more of the survivors. The rest survived for three days trapped in the plane before finally breaking out.

How would you be feeling at this point?

It is recommended that one stay with a plane after it crashes. In this case, they really didn't think they had anywhere they could go. The problem was that the plane was painted white and was resting on snow. They tried making emergency signals in the snow but had limited capabilities.

The group finally took action and decided to send four members to seek help. However, they waited several more weeks to allow the weather to warm up a bit. Assuming they had made it into Chile (they were actually still in Argentina), the direction they decided to head was west. However, a large mountain blocked the way (which should have been a hint they were still in the eastern part of the Andes). So they set out east, hoping a valley would curve around back to the west.

They came upon the tail section of the plane. Stripping it of whatever they found useful, they continued on the next day. However, they almost froze to death that night camping out in the open and were forced to retreat. They decided that perhaps they could use the batteries in the tail section of the plane to power the radio in the cockpit. However, the batteries were too heavy to carry back uphill to the main part of the plane. So they returned to their comrades. Several removed the radio and took it to the tail where they tried, fruitlessly, to transmit (different currents). This was another setback, where a flickering hope was snuffed out.

Lesson

Often during a crisis, bad things pile up.

This group experienced hearing about the cancellation of the search. Then they were hit by the avalanche that killed eight and buried the rest inside the fuselage for days before they were able to dig out.

Surviving those two events was difficult. I've seen well-trained, handpicked men, give up after experiencing a single disaster. This group was hit again and again. Not only did they not give up, they worked hard to survive and ultimately, decided to take matters into their own hands.

Cascade Five

Learning Survival the Hard Way.

The group had been traveling to a rugby match, not a survival exercise. They had very little in the way of equipment with which to deal with the high altitude and extreme cold. The next time on a plane, look around and think to yourself what would be useful in such circumstances. After you went through the snack cart, and used the thin blankets?

One of the members built hammocks for some of the injured. They learned that attaching seat cushions to their feet acted as a form of snowshoe. One of them made improvised sunglasses using the sun visors from the cockpit—snow blindness is a very real danger in this situation.

A critical need in any situation is water. I discuss this in detail in *The Green Beret Survival Guide*. One survivor worked out a way to use the sun to melt snow to provide water.

BOB MAYER

A second year medical student took charge of first aid after the doctor died. He improvised splints and braces using parts of the shattered airplane.

Knowing no one was searching for them any more, and devastated by the avalanche, the survivors realized the only way out was for someone to get rescuers to come to them. This meant a trek through the mountains to civilization. Wrongly believing they were near the western side of the Andes, they thought their best chance was to send some people west. However, their experience sending people to the tail of the plane, made them realize that no one could survive the night exposed to the elements. While daytime temperatures rose above freezing, at night they were well below and the barren terrain precluded finding any sort of shelter.

They took quilted insulation from the tail section of the plane and began to sow pieces together to make a large sleeping bag that three people could get in. The insulation, combined with the warmth generated by three people made a rescue expedition possible.

As they were completing the sleeping bag, another survivor died. This made even the most hesitant member accept that an expedition needed to be sent to find aid.

LESSON: Field expediency requires a positive outlook and a willingness to look at all resources with a different mindset.

I am serious when I suggest looking around the next time you are on a plane and think about how the pieces and parts could be used for survival. Look at your car. Do you have a grab-n-go bag in it? I go into preparation in detail in *The Green Beret Survival Guide*. But on top of preparation, a survival mindset is key. Improvisation and pooling the various skills of the group (even something so mundane as sewing!) can be the difference between life and death.

*Note in the following excerpt from The Green Beret Survival Guide, where the survivors of Flight 571 used the various aspects of **The Acronym to Remember: SURVIVAL***
*In Special Forces we're taught that the word **Survival** provides you with the first letters of the keys you need.*
S - Size up the situation, your surroundings, yourself, and your equipment.
U - Use All Your Senses; Undue Haste Makes Waste
R - Remember Where You Are
V - Vanquish Fear and Panic
I - Improvise
V - Value Living
A - Act Like the Natives
L - Live by Your Wits, But for Now, Learn Basic Skills

S - Size up the situation, your surroundings, yourself, and your equipment.

There are two ways to take this: one is in preparation and the other is in the actual situation. For preparation, you size up your potential situations by doing an Area Study, which will we go through in detail in Chapter 4.

In the actual situation, the key is to focus on what exactly is the threat? This might seem obvious, but consider the situation in Japan in 2011. The initial event was the earthquake. That, however, wasn't the primary threat. The resulting tsunami caused much more devastation. And following that, the problems at the nuclear plants presented immense issues that are still having an effect.

Size up your surroundings.
When in a situation, tune in to the environment.

Have you ever spent a night alone, out in nature?

Most people haven't. But if you do, you will soon realize that you are part of a system. This is key to survival. You don't want to fight your environment; you want to work with it. There is a pattern to nature. In an urban environment there are also patterns. Make note of the patterns and also focus on any time the pattern is disturbed.

One thing that always struck me was that no matter where we went in the world, no matter how hard we tried to hide, the locals always knew we were there. Because our presence was abnormal. They sensed it. We weren't part of the normal pattern. You have to do the same with your environment.

Size up yourself.

Have you been hurt or wounded? Often, in the initial rush of a trauma, we miss potentially lethal injuries. We'll discuss emergency first aid later, but you must take the time to assess your physical condition. For gun shot wounds, the exit wound can offer be more dangerous than the entrance wound, but often people don't look for it.

Keep yourself healthy. Dehydration, which we'll cover under water, is a major problem that can easily be avoided. Notice how this is emphasized in The Hunger Games. The first piece of advice the mentor gives to the two candidates from his district is to find water. We can survive quite a while without food, but water is critical. Cold and wet are also enemies that you have to monitor and deal with.

Size Up Your Equipment

What do you have? What can you get? What condition is your equipment in? A lot of this will be covered under preparation, but some situations might require field expediency. What do you have that is necessary and what can you do without? People have been killed in natural disasters by trying to carry too much stuff with them. During the tsunami in Japan many people died while they tried to pick up what they felt were irreplaceable items. Some people even went back to their houses after initially evacuating and died. The most important things are people, not memorabilia or jewels or money.

U - Use All Your Senses, Undue Haste Makes Waste

Use all your senses. A key trait, which mystifies many people, is called 6th sense. Great point men in the army are valued for this trait. They'll be leading a patrol along a trail and suddenly stop. Something has alerted them, but they can't pinpoint it right away. We all have 6th sense, but most people don't pay attention to it. 6th sense is one or more of your other 5 senses picking up something real and alerting your subconscious. You actually saw or smelled or felt something, but didn't consciously register it. Trust that feeling. Focus and move whatever it is to your conscious mind.

Unless you are in imminent danger, slow down and think things through. Panic is a killer. If you don't think and plan, you could do the wrong thing and in some cases a "no do-over" action, which is usually fatal. Don't take an action or move just for the sake of doing something. Every action and movement must have a purpose.

R - Remember Where You Are

Know your location at all times. We'll go over traditional map reading later in this book because too many people have become reliant on GPS. Most don't even have physical road maps in their cars any more. We'll also discuss field expedient direction finding techniques.

Stay oriented. Often you can use significant terrain features for that, whether it be a coastline, a mountain range, a river. They can also give you boundaries. One of the things that didn't make sense in The Road was that they were supposed to be moving south all the time, yet sometimes the ocean was on their left and sometimes it was on their right.

(And for frack's sake, don't use a shopping cart to carry your gear! In essence, speaking as a novelist, it was a plot device that forced them to stay on the Road).

Make sure everyone in the group is oriented. Make sure you know who has the map and compass. And make sure the map, inside a waterproof case, and compass are tied off to your body with a 'dummy' cord. Never rely on others to know where you're located. If you are moving, make note of key terrain features and water sources.

Remember, water sources are where game congregates and usually have fish in them, so they are also food sources.

An experienced mountaineer, during my training at the International Mountain Climbing School, said a key to his surviving situations where others perished, was that while going up the mountain, he always looked back. He wanted to see what it would look like when he was coming down the mountain. More people get lost and killed coming down the mountain than going up.

Also make note of hide positions. In certain survival situations, you might not want to be found by others. In Panic in the Year Zero, the father of the family makes the decision to leave their comfortable camper and live in a cave, over the objections of his family. The couple who then squat in the camper are later found murdered, because it was too easy to find.

A key concept to survival is to accept there are times you are going to be very uncomfortable.

Uncomfortable is better than dead.

V - Vanquish Fear and Panic

Fear and panic kill. You need to understand your basic personality type. If you have anxiety disorder, you definitely need to team up with someone who doesn't have it. Panic and fear keep you from making the right decisions. You're reacting, instead of acting.

Don't let your imagination run too far in a fatalistic direction, much like the one soldier in Aliens who kept screaming "We're all going to die." You don't want someone like that on your team.

Think about times in your life when you were in a crisis. How did you react? How did those people you want on your team react in a crisis? How someone reacts in a crisis gives you a very good idea of someone's core personality type.

Panic and fear also drain your energy. You're not focused on what needs to be done; you're focused on what could possibly go wrong. One way to help lower fear and panic is to be prepared, have a plan, and practice aspects of survival training so you build your confidence.

I noted before that fear serves a purpose, but too much fear can paralyze.

I - Improvise

Look at the things around you with a different mindset in a survival situation. What might have one particular use in civilization can have a very different use in a survival situation.

However, I recommend against using a shopping cart as a means for carrying your gear as in The Road. Also, there really was no need for a rear-view mirror on the shopping cart. Think of the core flaw of using the shopping cart (besides being a dumb conveyance): they needed to avoid others, yet by using the cart, they had to stay on The Road. Where others would be.

No matter how well prepared you are, in an extended emergency, some of your gear will wear out. How can you use other objects around you? We'll cover some readily available objects and how they can be turned into other useful tools.

V - Value Living

Two men with similar wounds. One lived and one died. What was the difference? The one who lived wanted to with every atom of his being. The one who died succumbed to his fear and pain. He didn't value his life enough.

We tend to be creatures of comfort. Civilization has advanced to the point where few people have the day to day survival skills most had just a few generations ago. We buy our food prepared and pre-packaged. Our water comes from a tap. Electricity is taken as a given, rather than a precarious luxury.

One thing I have seen is that when people are willing and value living, they adapt surprisingly quickly. Most of our life consists of habits. When we are forced to change our habits, we adopt new ones. It is generally said it takes 21 days for a new habit to take hold. That's not very long at all in the big scheme of things.

No matter how hard it gets, never quit.

A - Act Like the Natives

If you are out of your natural environment, then observe those around you, both human and animal. Those that are native to the area have adapted to it. What do they eat? Where do they get their food and water? Are there places they avoid? What are their customs *and habits? Remember, even customs that seem very strange, often have a very practical root.*

Watching animals is key. They also need water, food and shelter. Animals can also be an alert for the presence of other humans. And they can alert others to your presence.

If you are a stranger, gain rapport with the locals. Treat them with respect. If you've ever seen the movie Naked Prey you can see the results of insulting the locals. That movie is an excellent example of a man with a burning desire to live no matter what the obstacles.

L - Live by Your Wits, But for Now, Learn Basic Skills

Reading this book isn't enough. There are skills you need to practice now, actions you need to rehearse before having to use them in an emergency. I will highlight these skills as we go through the book. Again, preparation is the key to success, both in terms of equipment and training.

Cascade Six

A 10-Day Trek for Rescue.

One day short of two months after the crash, armed with their sleeping bag and supplies scraped together, three members set out due west, heading up the mountain. At night, they huddled together in the sleeping bag, something any soldier who has gone through winter Ranger can assure you is not unusual.

Make your buddy smile.

From personal experience in repeated Winter Warfare training exercises with the 10th Special Forces Group (Airborne), I can tell you moving uphill, above the tree line, in snow, is brutal, even if you have skis, and they didn't.

It took them three days to make it to the top of the mountain, which, by the way was 15,260 feet high.

Once more, there was only despair. As far as the eye could see to the west were more mountains.

Realizing the road ahead was much longer and tougher than anticipated, and their supplies would not last the three of them, they sent one of their team back. It took him only one hour to slip and sled his way back to the crash site, giving you an idea of the power of gravity, both negative and positive.

The remaining two men, Nando Parrado and Roberto Cannessa, continued on.

Seven days after leaving the plane, they finally descended below the snowline, following a river to the west. They spotted a 'cowboy' on the other side of the raging water and signaled for help.

Thus, on day 70, these two men were rescued.

Lesson

The human spirit can overcome the most difficult terrain and weather.

Ten days in snow, freezing cold, and starving, is more than enough to make the average person curl up in a ball and die. As we saw in book I with the Donner Party, some did. Here, though, these two men, bravely kept going.

Final Event

Rescue.

It took two more days to get the rest of the survivors off the mountain.

This story of survival has been tainted by the sensationalism of the cannibalism, but lost in that is the unbelievable will of these people to survive, particularly Parrado and Cannessa.

Lesson: Perseverance needs to actually be more tenacious in the face of repeated setbacks.

Take action when necessary. When they realized they weren't going to be rescued, they didn't give up. They took action. Even the Donner Party sent the 'Forlorn Hope' of snowshoers up into the pass when they realized they had to.

This event, the survivors of Flight 571, is a resounding case of the power of people to survive in the direst of circumstances.

THE RULE OF SEVEN
Shit Doesn't Just Happen

I had to get your attention, just like engineers, soldiers, pilots, astronauts, passengers, policemen, firemen, etc. need to get someone's attention just before a catastrophe occurs in order to either prevent the event or save lives. And engineers, systems analysts, workers, and managers have to get the attention of others in order to point out cascade events that, if unchecked, will lead to a catastrophe.

Consider the meaning of the phrase shit happens. Saying *"shit happens"* indicates events are random, have no meaning and there is no accountability or responsibility. It indicates such events could just as easily happen again and there's nothing we can do about them.

Bullshit.

This series is about catastrophes and disasters and tragedies and how to avoid them, mitigate their effects and learn from them. As you will see studying seven significant events, they didn't just happen, and the people and organizations involved weren't completely helpless victims. Taking the attitude shit happens is potentially fatal for the future. It ignores painful and tragic lessons from the past. If we're going to make the deaths and suffering of victims to mean anything, we must learn from them.

The bottom line is we can predict and prevent many catastrophes because almost every one has a man made factor, a cascade event, involved. In other words, we have control over whether shit happens. But it means changing a complacent mindset, getting rid of delusional thinking, and viewing the world around us in a different way.

Because shit doesn't just happen.

Why write this book?

Because I've made mistakes.

We all have. And some of us have made mistakes that contributed, either completely or in some percentage, to a *no-do-over*. This is an event where you can't go back and change the result. There has been an irrevocable event. Often these involve death or permanent injury/wounding. You can't undo those.

Soldiers understand this because the environment in which we operate is full of no-do-overs. I'll discuss why Special Forces are called Masters of Chaos later on, but even as Masters, we only control what we control. The best-trained, best equipped, soldier in the world is still only one piece of the entire picture.

That's the part we have to focus on; what we have control over. Our lives play out with many events and tragedies that are beyond our control, but in which we have some input, some effect. That's what this book highlights, showing you catastrophes step by step, and how each step teaches us something.

There aren't bad people in these catastrophes (mostly). They might have made some wrong decisions, but we all have, and the value we can place on them is to learn from them. Sometimes, many of the victims were innocent and not responsible, but we must focus on those who are responsible and in charge and made the key decisions. Or didn't make a key decision.

I can look back and have to examine where my part was; where my human error, my lack of focus, my wrong thinking, poor decision-making and ignorance, entered into things. There are things I might not have been able to prevent, but if I don't examine my role, I'll never become better at what I do and a better person. And deep inside, I wonder what I could have prevented.

That is why this book exists.

When I was young I watched the movie

No Highway In The Sky starring Jimmy Stewart. It's about an engineer who fears the first jet-engine commercial airliner will crash because of metal fatigue. He's so convinced he's right, even though everyone else thinks he's wrong, that he retracts the landing gear while the plane is parked on the runway to prevent it from taking off. Of course, by the end of the movie he's proven right.

But of more interest, three years after the movie, the first jet passenger plane, the de Havilland Comet had two fatal crashes. The cause: metal fatigue.

Then I went to West Point and subsequently volunteered for the Special Forces (Green Berets). As I'll describe in the Why Listen To Me section, both of these experiences had a profound effect on the way I view the world around me. Operating in the covert world leads one to have a paranoid perspective where shit doesn't just happen, it's expected, and we have to deal with it.

I've written quite a few novels based on my experiences, but also some nonfiction books. *The Green Beret Survival Guide* is full of not only survival information, but also stories about survival events. In a way, this book is an expansion of those types of individual stories to larger catastrophes. *Who Dares Wins: Special Operations Strategies for Success* is where I apply what I learned and taught in Special Operations to the civilian world. As we'll see in the following disasters, expertise in areas such as communication, goal-setting, leadership, character, motivation, etc. all play a role.

Finally, my wife (who is terrified of flying) and I became very interested in a television show titled *Seconds From Disaster*, which aired on National Geographic. Over the seasons it covered just about every plane crash and numerous other disasters. And we noticed a startling commonality. No plane crash just happened. There was always a series of mistakes, miscalculations, negligence and other events leading up to those final seconds and the disaster. Which led us to develop the . . .

The Rule of 7: no crash happens in isolation or as the result of a single event. It requires a minimum of 7 things to go wrong in order for an airplane to crash. And one of those 7 is always human error. It might not be the primary cause, but it is always a contributing factor.

This book will show you how the Rule of 7 applies not just to plane crashes, but also to catastrophes across a spectrum of widely different events, from a ship sinking to a battle, to an emigrant party in the wilderness to tulips and a housing bubble.

What can we learn from 7 catastrophes that are relevant to us and could very well save your life and that of others?

We are more powerful than we believe in the face of catastrophe.

A catastrophe involving humans does not happen in isolation.

In fact, with enough knowledge and preparation, many individuals and organizations can avoid catastrophes altogether, and if caught in one, survive.

Thus, this book is about 7 catastrophes, utilizing the Rule of 7 to show you at least 7 contributing events to each catastrophe and how each one could have been avoided.

That is the purpose of this book.

Three Reasons To Listen To Me

I trained for, lived in, and succeeded in a chaotic environment in two careers: As a Special Operations soldier and making a living as a novelist.

I don't have a PhD in engineering or an MBA (I do have an MFA). I did earn a perfect score on the Systems Engineering final at West Point, but I majored in psychology. I have a unique background, having graduated the Military Academy, served in the Infantry and Special Forces including commanding an A-Team, being a battalion operations officer, and taught at the JFK Special Warfare Center and School, and am a best-selling author in the creative field of fiction and the practical field of non-fiction. I'm also a consultant using my Who Dares Wins paradigm applying Special Forces strategies and tactics to a variety of businesses and organizations.

Here are the three reasons my expertise contributes to this subject:

Reason One
West Point Trains One For,
And Special Operations Functions In,
Catastrophe

Catastrophe planning in the civilian world is primarily the province of engineers and management. The problem with that is engineers and management are trained for, plan for, and work in a controlled environment (what they think is a controlled environment). So delusion events are outside their comfort zone; aberrations. In fact, as we will see, engineers and managers are often trained to be blind to cascade events. Their training and work environment normally does not reward focusing on cascade events, but rather punishes it.

West Point is an extraordinarily controlled environment. Things run almost perfectly there; so much so that graduates often have problems adjusting to the 'real' Army they go into. But West Point also has over 200 years of experience training leaders and preparing soldiers for war. This accumulation of institutional knowledge is inculcated in cadets in a high-pressure cauldron of mental, physical and emotional stress for four years.

Of course, sometimes it doesn't take, as we will see with one of the events we cover in this book that focuses on one of our more notorious graduates.

Special Operations soldiers train for war. War is called controlled chaos; an incessant series of cascade events. War might be considered the ultimate catastrophe and combat a final event. In order to prepare for this final event, Special Operations soldiers train for, plan for, and work in a chaotic environment every day.

Mentally, the most difficult training I went through was Robin Sage, the final exercise in the Special Forces Qualification Course. Robin Sage is where a team of students is sent into isolation, and then infiltrates into the North Carolina countryside to conduct a guerilla warfare exercise. A critical component of Robin Sage is to put prospective Green Berets in lose-lose scenarios. This is a training scenario where there is no 'right' solution. Rigid minds are often unable to think creatively while under stress and lose-lose training quickly determines someone's capabilities.

Thinking outside of the immediate situation is important in preparing for and averting catastrophes. Do you remember in the Star Trek movie (*Wrath of Khan*) when Captain Kirk talks about being at Star Fleet Academy and being the only officer to have passed the *Kobayashi Maru* simulator program? The basic problem and the opening of the movie was set up this way: A Star Fleet ship, which the student commands, is patrolling near the neutral zone. A distress call is received from a disabled Federation vessel inside the neutral zone. An enemy warship is approaching from the other side. A vessel more powerful than the one the student commands. The choices seem obvious: ignore the distress call (which violates the law of space) or go to its aid (violating the neutral zone) and face almost certain destruction from the enemy vessel. As you can see, both choices are bad.

What Kirk did was sneak into the computer center the night before he was scheduled to go through the simulation and change the parameters so that he could successfully save the vessel without being destroyed. Would you have thought of that? Was it cheating? If you ain't cheating you ain't trying. It's not cheating when it succeeds.

A key to lose-lose training is you get to see how someone reacts when they are wrong or fail. Lose-lose training is a good way to put people in a crisis. Frustration can often lead to anger, which can lead to failure or enlightenment.

If a catastrophe struck, whom would you want at your side helping you? A doctor? Lawyer? Policeman? Engineer? MBA? Teacher? While they all have special skills, I submit that the overwhelming choice might well be a Special Forces Green Beret. Someone trained in survival, medicine, weapons, tactics, communications, engineering, counter-terrorism, tactical and strategic intelligence, and with the capability to be a force multiplier.

Most important, you want someone who has been handpicked, survived rigorous training, and has the positive mental outlook to not only survive, but also thrive in chaos, and knows how to be part of a team. Green Berets have been called Masters of Chaos. Every Green Beret is also a leader.

A key to dealing with catastrophes is leadership, not management. Often, in order to deal with a cascade event, leadership and courage are needed to go against a culture of complacency and fear. As we will see in each catastrophe, fear is a factor in at least one, if not more, cascade events. This fear runs the gamut from physical fear, to job security fear, to social fear, to physical fear. Few people want to be the 'boy who cries wolf' even when they see a pack of wolves. What's even harder is when we're the only one who sees the wolf in sheep's clothing.

I've written this book to help individuals and organizations avoid catastrophes, but I come at it from a different direction as a former Special Operations soldier. In the Special Forces (Green Berets) the key to our successful missions was the planning. The preparation. In isolation we war-gamed as many possible catastrophe situations we could imagine for any upcoming mission and prepared as well as we could for them. In fact, we expected things to go wrong, a very different mindset from that of engineers and management. We were firm believers in Murphy's Law: What can go wrong, will. In other words: Shit will happen.

Our job was to deal with it.

Reason Two
Less Is Better

This book is short and to the point. There are thousands of catastrophes I could have drawn from. I focus on these seven in this first book in order to give focus. Each is representative of a type of catastrophe. We can extrapolate the catastrophe to similar circumstances, but the key is to understand the overall concept of having a catastrophe mindset. Further books in this series will cover other catastrophes, with the lessons learned from each. As we go through more and more catastrophes we will see patterns. Since there are an infinite number of possible scenarios and cascade events, the goal is to learn to adopt a mindset rather than focus on specific solutions.

I don't go into much detail on each of the cascade events of each disaster. I list them, with a timeline, a brief explanation, and then a comment on the lesson learned from each cascade event leading up to the final event. The goal is to have a cumulative impact on your mindset as you go through catastrophe after catastrophe. This book is about a mindset because there is no way to cover every possible scenario. Each of you is in a unique situation. You must learn the catastrophe mindset and then apply it to your unique environment and circumstances and also be prepared for the unexpected because catastrophes often strike in unexpected ways.

What can go wrong inevitably will.

There are also 'asides' throughout this book marked by the Special Forces patch and italicized font. Feel free to skip them; they are interesting tidbits from personal experience or other events that I've put in as an added benefit.

I chose some significant catastrophes that almost everyone has heard of. (Unfortunately, the two teenage girls behind me when I went to see the movie *Titanic* were not aware the ship was going to sink. They were quite distraught when it did.) These are events that echo in our collective consciousness.

Reason Three
The HALO Effect

HALO isn't the video game: It stands for High Altitude Low Opening parachuting. We jump above 25,000 feet and fall. A long way. Then open the parachute at a low altitude.

This is the term I use when I consult for a business foreign to me, like IT. When I walk in to an IT company I know pretty much nothing about how they do things (I know how to turn my computer on, but that's about it). But that actually gives me an advantage because I have no pre-conceived notions about how things should be done. I am not going to reinvent the wheel, the way most organizations periodically do. I am thinking outside the box because I was never in the box to begin with. This is what I mean when I say step back from your environment and look at it with a completely different perspective: one of potential catastrophe.

For potential catastrophes, as we will see, an outside perspective often lacks the dangerous, closed mindsets that often permeate organizations. An outsider is also free of internal pressures, politics, and critiques. An outsider can see delusion events as possible cascade events. An outsider is free of the chain of command/management and is freer to express concerns. An outsider is trained differently than insiders and has a different perspective.

DEFINITION: Lose-lose scenarios: A training scenario where there is no 'right' solution.

DEFINITION: Catastrophe mindset: Expecting that what can go wrong; will.

DEFINITION: HALO: Looking at something from 'outside the box' giving a fresh and unique perspective.

Three Benefits of Catastrophe Thinking, Planning & Preparing

As a Green Beret, I was focused on two main reasons for catastrophe planning and preparation. As a writer, I learned about a third, more subtle benefit of catastrophe planning, in order to have a successful career in a field where 99% of those entering eventually fail.

You Catastrophe Plan for three reasons

1. To avoid the catastrophe. Since at least one of the six cascade events is human error, if we plan and prepare adequately, we can delete the human error cascade event from the situation, thus avoiding the final event.

2. To have a plan, equipment, training etc. in place in case the catastrophe strikes. If we project out possible final events, we can prepare for their eventuality. I am adamant that preparation is critical, even more so than actual actions during the final event. It is too late when we reach a final event to prepare for it. Even the best-trained individual will be overwhelmed by a final event if they have not prepared for it. In the last catastrophe we cover in this book, you'll see how the fact someone planned for possible catastrophes helped avert a terrible final event.

3. To give you peace of mind in day-to-day living so you don't constantly have to worry about potential catastrophes because you are prepared for them. This allows you to experience a higher quality of life. You've done your best to avoid the catastrophe, making the likelihood that much less. And you've done your best to prepare for the catastrophe, so you can focus on other things. Too many people worry about potential catastrophes without preparing; this is a fundamental failure and fuels fear. Fear feeds on itself and is debilitating. Often, extreme fear can bring about an event that would have never occurred otherwise. Confident people are prepared people.

7 Ways To Prevent Catastrophes

ONE
Have A Preparation Mindset

The key is to accept that shit doesn't just happen. As you now know, most catastrophes are the result of cascade events. The origins of future catastrophes lie in our past and in our present.

When my A-Team traveled, my engineers would always be looking at things they saw with a different perspective than most people. When they saw a bridge, they were mentally calculating how to blow it up. When they saw a stream, they were thinking how to dam it and provide a water supply to villagers. My weapons men would look at terrain for fields of fire for direct and targeting points for indirect fire weapons. To be a survivor, you have to look at your environment in terms of what you can use and what can be a threat, which requires you to assume a different mindset for a while.

The best way to prevent a catastrophe is to plan for it. If engineers at NASA had not planned for the unlikely 'lifeboat' possibility, the crew would have never made it back.

In order to plan for it, you must do the next six things.

TWO
Focus

Pay attention, both to immediate events and surroundings, and the past. We generally think in one of two different ways: a big picture thinker or a detail thinker.

Both types are needed. Understand yourself and those in your organization.

A big picture thinker can see patterns. This person can put the pieces together in order to see trends that could lead to catastrophe.

A big picture thinker would see the flow of history regarding bubbles and have known the housing bubble was inevitable.

Unfortunately, a big picture thinker might miss the key details that make up those trends.

A big picture thinker might have passed over that single sentence in the book about the Hastings Cutoff and focused on the fact the California Trail was the way people had successfully been journeying to California.

Binoculars locked up on a huge ship like the *Titanic* is a pretty small detail at the time, but in retrospect that single event loom large.

And a detail thinker might miss how each piece is part of a larger tapestry.

For the New London Schoolhouse, some people certainly noted the ill students, but might not have been able to connect that with leaking gas.

For both types, they have to focus hard on the area they are lacking.

I'm a big picture thinker. So I've had to work very hard to focus on details. I've had to learn not to get upset when a detail is pointed out to me that I haven't noticed. In fact, I've had to learn to focus on what I call an anger indicator. I always advise people that when they get angry, it's usually because they're hearing or seeing or experiencing a truth they don't want to.

When I get angry, I always try to focus on what exactly it is that is making me upset and in doing so I can often uncover key truths. The more an organization fights something, the more likely that something is going to be part of a cascade event.

More on this in **Who Dares Wins: Special Operations Strategies for Success.**

THREE
Conduct Area Studies

In Special Forces, prior to deploying to an Area of Operations, we conducted an Area Study of that location. You must conduct an Area Study of your Catastrophe Area of Operations (AO). Your home, your work, and any other locales where you spend a significant amount of time. When taking a trip, you should conduct a travel area study, examining the route you will take, your destination, and your route back.

There are so many cases where a thoughtful Area Study followed up by the appropriate preparations would have saved lives and avoided catastrophe. Prevention is more efficient than avoidance. Preparation is so much better than reacting.

Custer certainly would have benefited from an area study. At the very least, a better reconnaissance would have shown him what he was really up against.

The Donner Party put their lives on the line because of the words of a man who had not done an area study, but wrote as if he had.

Think about it. You live in a tsunami zone. Have you actually driven your evacuation route? How long does it take? Have you figured out the quickest escape route on foot, when an accident caused by terrified people blocks the road or everyone in your neighborhood fleeing on the same route creates a traffic jam? You work on the 90th floor of a skyscraper. Do you ever look around and ask yourself: how do I get out of here if the normal means of egress are blocked?

How close are you to the nearest military base? Nearest police station? Firehouse? Hospital? Even in day-to-day living, do you know where the closest emergency room is? How long it will take to get there? How quickly can an ambulance respond to your location?

You want to examine your environment for a lot of things. What can harm you? What can help you? What can hide you? What are your enabling factors? What are your disabling factors? What effect does your environment have on you? What effect will you have on it? In essence, an Area Study requires you to invest the time and energy on research.

For an A-Team, we conducted the Area Study in Isolation where we were locked up 24/7 in a secure compound. We'd bring in area

experts (CIA agents, State Department personnel, people who'd traveled there, locals, academics, etc.) to tell us about the environment we were heading into. This is a technique I recommend for businesses under my Who Dares Wins program.

Do a HALO study of your environment and organization.

An Area Study must combine with the catastrophe mindset to focus on what can go wrong will go wrong!

More on this in both the Survival Guide and WDWSOS

FOUR
Use the CARVER Formula

CARVER is a formula we use in Special Forces to assess targets for specific missions. It is the way we find critical nodes and the places where catastrophe is most likely to happen; or be made to happen.

You can apply the CARVER Formula to your organization by considering it a target for catastrophe and then reverse think it. As a novelist, I start a thriller by taking the bad guy's point of view and come up with his or her nefarious plan. As a catastrophe preventer, you have to take the point of view opposite to what you're used to: how can my organization, ship, plane, building, business, etc. fall apart? Be destroyed? By both man-made and natural forces? Once you figure those possibilities out, you can then work to prevent cascade events.

Here is CARVER, which is a framework you can use:

CRITICALITY: How important is the target? What are the critical nodes of the target? For example, to put a port out of commission for a while, a critical node might be the shipping channel. Or the cranes that load and off-load cargo. Or Pearl Harbor's fuel depot (Book 2 in this series).

ACCESSIBILITY: Can the target be gotten to? How? Can the part of the target that is to be destroyed be accessed? There are often many critical nodes, but some are more easily attacked than others, thus making it more vulnerable.

RECOGNIZABILITY: Can the target be recognized? Can the critical nodes be located?

VULNERABILITY: Will the team have the capability to actually destroy the target? For example, a dam requires a tremendous amount of force to breach, normally more than a team could carry in. But to overcome this limitation, a team could use a laser designator to guide bombs or cruise missiles in to a target. Never accept limitations at first—there are usually ways to overcome them. How vulnerable are your critical nodes?

EFFECT: What effect outside of the target itself, will the damage have? For example, a team might have the mission to destroy a bridge that the enemy uses to carry supplies over. But will destroying that bridge have too large a negative effect on the population?

RECUPERABILITY: How long will it take to fix the damage done to the target? How quickly can you recover from a cascade event or even a final event?

CARVER is a way of looking at the details that make up the big picture.

FIVE
Have a 10th Man

"When you find yourself on the side of the majority, it is time to pause and reflect." Mark Twain.

When I was watching *World War Z*, one scene really struck me. When the lead character goes to Israel and finds they've already built a wall around Jerusalem to protect themselves from the zombies. He asks how did they know to build the wall before the zombies arrived?

The answer is the 10th Man.

While it is fiction (remember plane attacks on buildings were postulated in fiction well before 9-11), the concept is one that is intriguing for organizations to implement. It can help overcome the inertia of bureaucracy.

Having been badly surprised during the Yom Kippur War in 1973, the Israeli military has focused on preventing a similar catastrophe in the future.

In World War Z, the series of events went this way:

Ten days before the zombies spread into Israel, and it was public, the military received a vague email from an Indian general mentioning 'zombies'. Naturally, pretty much everyone blew this off. But the 10th Man policy had been enacted where, if 9 people agree, then the 10th man must disagree regardless of how crazy it sounds. In this case, they acted on that disagreement, building a wall for a zombie invasion only one person thought might happen.

The 10th Man concept is an excellent way to build a contrarian point of view into an organization. Instead of being the boy who cried wolf, the 10th Man is expected to cry wolf.

But there's more to it than that.

The 10th Man just doesn't disagree; he/she must posit a different take on the situation, along with supporting evidence. This position must be listened to with an open mind. By arguing the 10th Man's points, what often happens is an alternative possibility is uncovered that no one considered. It's a way of war-gaming possible catastrophes.

A 10th Man in the rear of the plane during Kegsworth would have pointed out that the wrong engine had been shut down.

SIX
Conduct After Action Reviews

The seven catastrophes were covered in this book in a form of an After Action Review. The hardest AARs to conduct are when things go well. To incorporate catastrophe thinking into a successful event.

Also, a key is to focus on any deviation, any potential problem that went away: i.e. a delusion event.

An organization that won't look closely at itself is doomed to keep doing the same things wrong again and again until eventually the events cascade to a catastrophe.

Because simulated combat exercises are so difficult to observe and judge, the military designed the AAR to help the participants figure out what happened. It was only in the late 90s that the business world began picking up the concept, most likely a result of Army officers filtering into the civilian world and bringing what they had learned with them. A Harvard Business School professor wrote an article about it in the Harvard Business Review in 1993. The most critical aspect of having an effective AAR is honesty. The first, and most important, question to be answered is, "was the goal or mission accomplished?" Given that your goal or mission was originally stated clearly in one sentence, the answer should be clear.

I have read several business books where it is said an AAR should not judge success or failure. I disagree with that. Why not? The theory is that focusing on success or failure will cause emotional conflict—if that's the case, then so be it. We succeed. We fail. We learn, adjust and move on. Successful people have to break through the conflict that comes with not succeeding all the time. In order to uncover delusion events, extreme honesty is needed.

One time when I was jumpmastering, during the pre-jump briefing I forgot to ask an important question: If anyone there hadn't parachuted in a specified amount of time. Everyone participating was Special Ops and experienced so I screwed up by not asking a question in the SOP. It turned out there was a new man in the unit who hadn't jumped in years. Instead of heading out for a jump, he should have been heading to jump refresher training. During the AAR, I had to bring up my screw-up even though there hadn't been a problem. The issue was there could have been a problem.

If the answer is yes, you achieved your goal, then pat yourself on the back, then see what fine-tuning needs to be done and what potential catastrophes could occur if things didn't go quite right. Also, focus on any time words like "lucky" come up.

Steps for an effective AAR with a focus on preventing cascade and final events.

Review your plan. Did you follow your plan? If not, note the exceptions and variations you made. Did any rule breaking of the plan work? What didn't work?

Summarize the events as they occurred, using a detailed timeline, with no commentary. Just the facts. Build a complete timeline of action.

Focus on why each specific action was taken. Whether each step of the plan was followed, or deviated from (which is not necessarily a bad thing).

Give particular focus to when fear played a role in your actions—this is the most difficult part of the AAR, but the most critical—fear is most likely where your actions diverged from your plan.

Examine what role SOPs played. Did they work? Do they need to be revised?

Summarize areas of plan improvement and refinement, as well as alternative actions you could have taken to achieve a more successful result.

What were the lucky breaks during the activity?

When did you dodge the bullet?

What if we'd failed? What would have been the critical nodes where failure was most likely? How can we make sure those critical nodes aren't as vulnerable?

A key is to make hindsight, foresight.

Something to remember is there are over 1,000 near misses for every work accident that results in a serious injury or death. The more focus that is placed on near misses, the less common they become and the less likely a serious injury or death occurs.

After Action Reviews are worthless if they aren't used. They need to be made accessible to everyone and kept on file in a way they can easily be found. Too many organizations reinvent the wheel over and over because they don't learn from their own past. AARs are good ways to begin writing your SOPs.

SEVEN
Use Standing Operating Procedures

Standing Operating Procedures (SOPs) are anything written down that delineates how things should be done. They can serve many purposes. The key part of the first sentence of this paragraph is written down. Writing something down makes it real. It also makes it easily available. It reduces confusion and misunderstanding.

Every job I've ever done, I've ended up writing an SOP for it. Usually I do this because, surprisingly to me, no one before me did it, even when it was part of their job. I also did it so I could better understand what I was supposed to be doing.

When I finished my Special Forces training at Fort Bragg, I was issued orders assigning me to the 10th Special Forces Group (Airborne) at Ft Devens, MA. I was assigned as a team's executive officer. After being in-briefed by the team leader, he asked me if I had any questions. The first thing I did was ask him for the team's SOP, as I had been taught to do at Fort Bragg. I was surprised when he told me they didn't have one. He had explanations why they didn't need one, but ultimately, in retrospect, the primary reason was no one had taken the initiative to write one, because writing an SOP is a very time consuming process. It's a 'front-end'-'back-end' deal. You put the work in on the front end to save you considerably more time in the long run on the back end. Unfortunately, too often, people are overwhelmed up front and don't see the larger and long range picture.

When I took command of my own A-Team a few months later, once again, the first thing I asked was where was the team SOP. After my previous experience, I wasn't too surprised when I was told the team didn't have one written down. They 'knew' what they needed to do, I was told. Right. And even if they did, how was I supposed to 'know' it?

So I began writing the team SOP. Basically, I began formalizing what everyone said they 'knew'. I not only drew from my team members' expertise, I went to other teams and found those who did have SOPs and got copies. I went to the company headquarters and talked to the Sergeant Major who had extensive combat experience and got him to help, giving us some tips—seemingly small, but ones that could save your life in combat.

The team SOP when completed was rather detailed and a living document that we constantly refined as we tested concept in it and learned what worked and what didn't. The beginning of it was mine and my team sergeant's policy letters, spelling out our philosophy for leading the team.

My team sergeant was direct and to the point. Here were some of his choicer lines:

- Nothing is impossible to the man who doesn't have to do it.
- Smith & Wesson beats four aces.
- The latest information hasn't been put out yet.
- There are two types of soldiers– the steely eyed killer and the beady eyed minion.
- Here are some excerpts from mine:
- Most basic tenet of teamwork is honesty.
- With rank & privilege comes responsibility.
- Everyone is a leader.
- We do everything together.
- If you have a problem with someone with higher rank, let me know.
- Keep a positive attitude.
- Discipline stays at team level.
- Be on time.
- Keep your sense of humor. You'll need it.

After the policy letters, we then specified who on the team was responsible for what. We took much of this from the field manual for Special Forces that had this information. You can help yourself tremendously when writing an SOP to check out what is already out there. Someone, somewhere, probably wrote one just like what you want to write. It might well be buried in the file cabinets or on a thumb drive somewhere.

We then covered numerous tactical situations and codified how each team member would act. Then we would train on those SOPs until the actions became instinctual.

Sops Codify And Set Standards

When I was first published I attended a continuing education class on magazine writing. I didn't have plans to write articles, but I figured it was a form of writing so I would learn something. I was trying to get out of my tunnel vision. The instructor gave out a thin comb-bound booklet covering the material he was going to teach. I thought this was a good idea and when I was getting ready to teach my first writing class, I did the same.

Special Operations has always relied on SOPs. If you get a copy of the current US Army Ranger Handbook, which every good Infantry and Special Forces officer should be packing, in the very beginning is a list of Roger's Rules of Rangering. The first Rangers were formed in 1756 and Rogers wrote his rules in 1759 after three years of combat experience on the frontier. Some of these sound quite simple but they were learned, as many of the lessons in this book were, at the cost of blood:

Don't forget nothing.

Tell the truth about what you see and do.

When you're on the march, act the way you would if you were sneaking up on a deer. See the enemy first.

Don't never take a chance you don't have to.

When we camp, half the party stays awake while the other half sleeps.

Don't ever march home the same way. Take a different route so you won't be ambushed.

And so on—all very basic, but rules that are constantly violated every day by military forces. At the cost of blood.

Whatever your job is, you should have an SOP for it. And it should be written so that someone with no background can achieve a base level of functioning in the job for a short period of time. Other SOPs should lay out the way your organization works. The way things really work, not how you want someone to think they work.

SOPs are a great way to codify habits you want to develop and also list habits you want to avoid. Writing them down and posting them some place you can consistently see them helps keep you in the real world.

Failure to follow SOPs lays the groundwork for disaster, as is failing to study history.

SOPs should be followed, but also evaluated in the face of changing circumstances. SOPs are not written in stone. SOPs need to be checked every once in a while to make sure that they are applicable and that they are being followed. Having a nice looking binder with wonderfully written SOPs does you no good if you don't read them or follow them. And SOPs that are out of date can cause more harm than good. They should be constantly updated based on After Action Reviews.

I just read an interesting article that said that hospitals that use 10 item pre-surgery and post-surgery checklists cut their mortality rates in half. Simple things like: Is this the right patient? Is this the right surgery for this patient? Is this the correct arm to amputate? Have we accounted for all our equipment after the surgery?

It's not just the checklist—it's the added focus. There's a thing called the Hawthorne effect, which is that by simply observing something, you change the something, usually for the better. It was the fact that the people operating knew they were being observed during a test to see if the checklists worked, that improved things.

CONCLUSION

The wide range of catastrophes in this book give you a feel for the concept that disasters rarely happen in isolation.

The keys are:
- Remember the Rule of 7.
- A catastrophe is closer than you think.
- Watch for cascade events. Act when you see one.
- Beware delusion events.
- Catastrophe plan as needed.

Remember: Shit Doesn't Just Happen!

NON FICTION TITLES
BY BOB MAYER

The Green Beret Survival Guide

This is a book that can save your life and the life of those you love. Part of the proceeds will go to Special Operations Warrior Foundations. SOWF provides scholarships grants, education and family counsiling to the surviving children of special operations personnel who have died.

Who Dares Wins: *Special Operations Strategies for Success*

"Success in life—as in combat—has always demanded depth of character. Who Dares Wins reveals what it takes for you to move into the world of elite warriors and how their training developed that Can Do spirit and Special Forces ethos of excellence." Lewis C. Merletti: Director United States Secret Service (retired), Former Sgt 5th Special Forces Group (Vietnam); Cleveland Browns Executive Vice President & COO

Novel Writer's Toolkit: *From Writer to Successful Author*

"An invaluable resource for beginning and seasoned writers alike. Don't miss out."
#1 NY Times Best-Selling Author Terry Brooks

Write It Forward: *From Writer to Successful Author*

"Bob Mayer is a gifted writer and a generous teacher." #1
NY Times best-selling author Susan Wiggs

OTHER BOOKS

102 Solutions to Common Writing Mistakes
Writer's Conference Guide: Getting the Most of Your
Time and Money
How We Made Our First Million: The Complete Digital
Author

FICTION BOOKS BY BOB MAYER

THE CELLAR SERIES
Bodyguard of lies

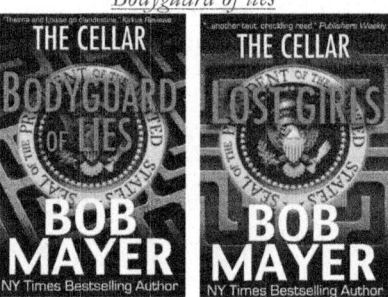

Praise for Bodyguard of Lies: "Thelma and Louise go clandestine." Kirkus Reviews

Praise for Lost Girls: " . . .delivers top-notch action and adventure, creating a full cast of lethal operatives armed with all the latest weaponry. Excellent writing and well-drawn, appealing characters help make this another taut, crackling read." Publishers Weekly

THE SHADOW WARRIOR SERIES

The Gate

"A pulsing technothriller. A nailbiter in the best tradition of adventure fiction." Publishers Weekly.

The Line

"Mayer has crafted a military thriller in the tradition of John Grisham's The Firm." Kirkus

THE GREEN BERET SERIES
An 8 book series featuring Dave Rile and Horace Chase

Eyes of the Hammer

"Exciting and authentic. Author Mayer, a Green Beret himself, gave me a vivid look at the world of the Army's Special Forces as they battle America's most deadly enemy. His portrayal of Green Beret operations and techniques takes you deep into the covert world of Special Operations as a you follow an A-Team into combat. Don't miss this one."
WEB Griffin

THE ATLANTIS SERIES

A 6 book Science Fiction Series

"Spell-binding! Will keep you on the edge of your seat. Call it techno-thriller, call it science fiction, call it just terrific story-telling." Terry Brooks, #1 NY Times Bestselling author of the Shannara series and Star Wars Phantom Menace

THE AREA 51 SERIES
A 9 book Science Fiction Series

When nine atmospheric crafts of unknown origin were discovered in the Antarctic in the late 1940s, the U.S. government established Area 51 to study the abandoned technology. Dr. Hans Von Seeckt, who is the only original member of the secret research committee, has observed the marvelous craft in flight and witnessed a fantastic array of bizarre, unexplained phenomena. But Dr. Van Seeckt fears that the technology of the mothership is beyond our scope and an explosive threat to the entire planet. He must race against time to unlock the secret of the ship--and to the origins of mankind itself.

THE NIGHTSTALKERS SERIES

Bob Mayer's *Nightstalkers* grabs you by the rocket launcher and doesn't let go. Fast-moving military SF action—just the way I like it. Highly recommended. -B.V. Larson

For more information on Bob Mayer please visit http://bobmayer.org or http://coolgus.com

ABOUT THE AUTHOR

Bob Mayer is a NY Times Bestselling author, graduate of West Point, former Green Beret (including commanding an A-Team) and the feeder of two Yellow Labs, most famously Cool Gus. He's had over 60 books published including the #1 series Area 51, Atlantis and The Green Berets. Born in the Bronx, having traveled the world (usually not tourist spots), he now lives peacefully with his wife, and said labs, at Write on the River, TN.

Made in the USA
Coppell, TX
21 August 2021